# Berhane
## The Peace Messenger

The extraordinary life of Berhane Woldegabriel,
Eritrean teacher, journalist and bridge-builder

Edited by

Ali Hindi, Amanda Woolley, Amanuel Yemane,
Peter Riddell

Published by
**The Endless Bookcase**
Suite 14, STANTA Business Centre, 3 Soothouse Spring,
St Albans, Hertfordshire, AL3 6PF

This is a collaborative work with contributions in the form of text and images from multiple authors each of whom retains copyright. The principle copyright holders are stated below. Any request for copyright permission should be directed via the publisher.

Photograph copyright holders are indicated by their initials: Ali Hindi (AH), Amanda Woolley (AW), Amanuel Yemane (AY), Christine Brown (CB), Peter Riddell (PR).

**Paperback edition**
Also available in multiple ebook formats

**ISBN: 978-1-914151-92-7**

Available from
www.theendlessbookcase.com

The views and opinions expressed in this book are those of the various writers and do not necessarily reflect the views of the editors. Although the editors and writers have made every effort to ensure that the information in this book is correct, the editors, writers and publisher do not assume and hereby disclaim any liability to any party for any loss, damage, or disruption caused by errors or omissions.

The editors request the understanding of contributors if their items have been separated into different parts of chapters, or different chapters, in order to observe the consistency of the narrative.

# Editors' bios

Ali Hindi was born in Eritrea, but his family left almost immediately. He lived in Saudi Arabia until 1989 when he came to the UK as a refugee. Ali met Berhane in 2008 and became a member of the EEPT (Eritrean Education and Publication Trust), where he played a role in organising all the events the EEPT held in cooperation with IofC (Initiatives of  Change). He also became a close friend of Berhane. Ali is a political analyst, specialising in African affairs. He is called on for interview by various television channels and media outlets. He is the Head of the African Study Unit in the Centre for Arab Progress.

 Amanda Woolley worked in London for over three decades in adult education. At Kensington and Chelsea College in 1993, she met Berhane as a colleague and they became partners for many years. Amanda's interest in Eritrea led her to do an MA in Asian & African History at SOAS. Her work in education included literacy teaching, developing innovative programmes at the Workers Educational Association (WEA), running an inner-city centre at Morley College and organising IT training at the Refugee Council. Amanda was the first manager of the Quaker Centre at Friends House. She now lives in West Yorkshire. Having retrained, she works part-time as a bereavement counsellor in a Lancashire hospice.

Amanuel Yemane was born and brought up in Eritrea. He was a freedom fighter for the independence of Eritrea, and came to the UK in 1997 as a refugee. Amanuel met Berhane in the summer of 2000 through mutual friends and remained a close friend and colleague at the EEPT, a charity co-founded by Berhane in the mid-'90s. He is a chartered accountant and works as Head of Finance for a digital marketing company in the City of London. He is also treasurer for the EEPT in his spare time. He lives with his family in Greenwich, South-East London.

Peter Riddell's journey towards his two decades of close collaboration with Berhane started when he joined a student delegation to Egypt in the early 1970's. It led to a 40-year association with British-Arab Exchanges, hosting Arab students and young professionals in the UK, and accompanying the return visits of their British peers. This experience made him painfully aware of the British  legacy of conflict and suffering in many countries. In response, he began to support outstanding peacemakers particularly in Africa and the Middle East. During the 1990s, Peter coordinated IofC's annual conferences on 'Agenda for Reconciliation' at Caux, Switzerland. Its weekly planning meetings took place in the IofC centre in London and it was there that his and Berhane's paths crossed...

# Dedication

The editors would like to dedicate this book to
Berhane's children:

Yemane, Medhanie, Fewien, Hadish and Jonathan,

his grandchildren, Raphael and Abigail,

and his sister Haimanot and her family.

# Table of Contents

## Chapter Six

# Interviews

**Chapter 1**

Amanda Woolley with Dimi Tomova

Amanda Woolley with Louis Leeson

**Chapters 2-4**

Amanuel Yemane with Haimanot Woldegabriel

**Chapter 3**

Amanda Woolley with Ali Hindi

# Acknowledgements

The editors would like to thank the following contributors:

Andy Gregg

Christine Brown

David and Elizabeth Locke

Dimi Tomova

Ghirmai Negash

Gillian Moyes

Goitom Mebrahtu

Haimanot Woldegabriel

Jim Baynard-Smith

Josephine Apira

Lajeel Abdirahman

Louis Leeson

Michael Bartlet

Mohamed Kheir Omer

Mohamed Sharif Mohamud

Nyeya Yen

Petros Tesfagiorgis

Solomon Ghebre-Ghiorghis

Stephen Yeo

Teame Mebrahtu

Tekeste Negash

Ursula Howard

Yacoub Idris

Yaseen Mohmad Abdalla

Yohannes Asmelash

The editors also thank:

- Yaseen Mohmad Abdalla for the book's title, Solomon Ghebre-Ghiorghis for the title of Chapter 2, and Mohamed Kheir Omer for the title of Chapter 4.

- Sudanow for permission to reproduce Berhane's writings from 'Sudanow' which appear in Appendix 1.

- Nyeya Yen for permission to reproduce Berhane's writings for 'Africa World Review' in Appendix 1.

- Carl French and Morgana Evans at our publishers, The Endless Bookcase, for their great professional service and their patience with us.

- Peter and Su Riddell for their kind hospitality in Oxford which enabled our face-to-face editing meetings.

- Family members and friends who have offered support in many ways throughout the process.

- Each other for a warm and positive collaboration that has enabled this complicated project to succeed.

We are grateful to include a passage from
'The give and take of writing: scribes, literacy and everyday life'
by Jane Mace.

# Editors' Introduction

Berhane Woldegabriel (1946-2020) was an Eritrean who left his country as a refugee in the 1970s. He then worked for thirteen years in Sudan, for the magazine 'Sudanow' and for the UNHCR (United Nations High Commission for Refugees) resettlement programme for refugees. He had to leave his adopted country after his writing offended the Sudanese government, and as a refugee for the second time, he settled in the UK in 1990.

Already an experienced teacher and journalist, he worked for nearly thirty years in London, mainly as an educator, translator, and interpreter. He also became a dedicated peacemaker, using his great political understanding and interpersonal skills as a facilitator and conciliator amongst Eritreans in the diaspora and within wider refugee communities.

Berhane died in October 2020 following a diagnosis, four months earlier, of a brain tumour. Until his illness took hold, and despite the COVID lockdown, he continued the reconciliation work he had become renowned for. His death was a shock to all who knew and loved him. Many of his friends and associates from his decades of work in Eritrea, Ethiopia, Sudan and the UK wrote and posted tributes and memories for Berhane.

The editors have linked many of these tributes with a description of Berhane's life and work. We hope in particular to show the unique skills that Berhane brought to his peace-making and to his work in general. As a person he is irreplaceable, but we have tried to describe his beliefs, approach and methods, which often went against the grain, in the hope it may encourage others to follow in his path. He was, in the words of his friend Mohamed Kheir Omer, 'a noble universal human being'.

This book provides a narrative of Berhane's life rather than being a biography. Although some recollections are intimate and heartfelt, it does not give a detailed account of his personal life. We have tried to avoid hagiography and give a rounded view of Berhane. Although he could be unpredictable in his approach to life and arrangements, we remember him as a lovable and modest man, noted for his warmth, erudition and wit. He had great insight, and the gift of being able to provide subtle encouragement to his many friends and to the groups he supported and developed. He loved people regardless of nationality and creed.

The first part of this book is about Berhane's life and work. The second part includes four examples of Berhane's journalism, the London Declaration of June 2020, and an essay by Professor Tekeste Negash, written specially for the book and dedicated to Berhane.

# Eulogy

## *Dr Teame Mebrahtu*

### On behalf of all Berhane's friends in the UK

I have known Berhane for over a quarter of a century, as a displaced fellow Eritrean in the UK. Since then, we have had opportunities to know each other better and to deliberate on issues of national concern ranging from the politico-social to cultural and educational arenas.

The eulogy in Tigrinya highlights that Berhane was a man of diverse talents and abilities. These included being or becoming a consummate journalist, a committed educator, a conflict-resolver, a mouthpiece for the hapless Eritrean youth who perished in the sea at Lampedusa, a good listener and debater, a bridge-builder between and within communities (e.g. the Eritreans and the Sudanese in the diaspora as well as the ethnic minorities and the host society in the UK) and an empowerer of the voiceless and dispossessed diaspora youth.

When closely examined, these attributes and qualities reflect and demonstrate the underlying principles Berhane upheld as an individual and a professional. Some of these inherent values, as identified in the eulogy include justice, fairness, dedication, diligence, service to others, patience, empathy, listening without judgement and peace-making.

On the other hand, despite extolling his virtues, the poem gently chastises Berhane for not hanging on long enough to see the re-birth of Eritrea, for being easily fooled by the perpetual liar and arch-enemy Mr Mort, and for his haste to depart from the midst of his family and friends without saying good-bye!

May His Soul Rest in Peace. Amen.

አብ ዕረፍቲ ናይ ኣቶ ብርሃነ ወልደገብርኤል ዝተገጥመ መግለጺ ሓዘንን ስንብታን

ንሓውና ብርሃን፡ ክንገብረሉ ናቱ

ክንምስክረሉ ኣቲ ቁም ነገሩ ፡ መንነቱ፨

ኣእዛንና፡ ከይኮርዓ

ኣዒንቲ፡ ከይደንበራ

ፍሕኛን፡ ኩሊትን፡ ሽፖሮ፡ ከይጀመራ

ልቢ ከይዘንገዐ፡ ሓንጎል ከይዘንበወ

ብእዋኑ፡ እንከሎ ጸሓይ ከይዐረበ፨

ብርሃን፡ ብርሃን፡ ወደቦይ ወልደገብርኤል

ዕባይ ጎዳይፍ ዕባይ ሰንበል

ወዲ ኣስመራ እታ ዓባይ ማእከል

ብቛሊሉ ዘይታለል ዘይህመል፨

ኣንታ ኣቦ ዓቕሊ ኣያ ልቦና

ዓብይ ሓው ወይዘሮ ሃይማኖት ሓፍትና

ዝሰልጠነ ብሙያ ምምህርና

ክእለቱ ዘመስከረ ገዲም ጋዜጠኛ

ምስጉን መምህር ናይ ቋንቋ ትግሪኛ፨

መምህር እወ ፍልጠቱ ዝልግስ

ታሪኽን፡ ባህልን፡ ሃገሩ፡ ዘውርስ

ሞራል ተመሃሮኡ ዝሓድስ፨

መምህር እወ፡ መምህር ንቕሓት፡

ኣቦ ዓቕሊ፡ ኣያ ጽንዓት

ኣቦ ትውፈት፡ ኣያ ትግሃት፨

ብርሃን፡ ብርሃን፡ እዚ ቐምነገርና

መሃንድስ፡ ጽቡቕን፡ ድልዱልን፡ ጉርብትና

ምስ ሱዳን፡ እዘም "ኣኸዋንና"

ምስ አፍሪቃውያን፡ እዞም አሕዋትና
ምስ እንግሊዛውያን መዕቆብትና።።
ሓላው ወሰን ህዝባዊ (ሲቪላዊ) መሰልና
አፈኛ፡ ናይቶም አብ ላምፐዱሳ ዝጠሓሉ ደቅና
ጠበቃ ናይ ኩሉ ሽጉር፡ ስደተኛ።።
አንታ ግዱስ ኤርትራዊ ዎሆይ በሃላይ
ደኺመ፡ ዘይብል ተጻዓራይ
ስለ ሓቅን፡ ፍትሕን፡ ተቓላሳይ
ስለ፡ ፍቅርን፡ ሥላምን፡ ተገዳሳይ።።
አንጻር ጭቆናን፡ መግዛእትን ተማጓታይ
ምውህሃድ፡ ዝመርጽ እንካብ ምፍልላይ
ርእይቶ፡ ወሃቢ፡ ሓሳብ ተቐባላይ
ብሓደ፡ ንስጉም፡ ንሕበር በሃላይ
ብዓዱን፡ ህዝቡን ተቘርቋራይ።።

አንታ ሓጺር በሪኽ ፍሽኽ ብሃላይ
ጨራቃይ፡ ተዋዛያይ
ብስልኪዶ፡ ረኪበካ አይነበርኩን፡ ብቓዳማይ፤
ድሓን፡ ምስ አማንዳ አብ ዕረፍቲኣየ፡ ዘሎኹዶ፡ አይበልካንን፡
ቆጸራ ዶኸ አይነበረናን
ስምምዕ ዶኸ አይገበርናን
ከንከይድ ንዓዲ ኩሉ ስደተኛ አኪብና
ከነገልግል ሃገርና
ጸግዒ፡ ከንኮኖ ንህዝብና
ከነማዕብላ ኤርትራና።።
እሞ፡ እንታይ ድኣ ረኺበካ፡ መን፡ ደፍአካ

ይግባኾ ድዩ፡ ድሓን ኩኑ፡ ከይበልካ

ከይተላዘብካ፡ ከይተመያየጥካ

ዝጀመርካዮ፡ ኣብ መድረኽ ከየብጻሕካ

ጻማ ጻዕርኻ ከይረኸብካ

ዝተላዕጠጠ፡ ሽግር ናይ ዓድኻ ተንቲንካ ከይፈታሕካ

ትንሣኤ ሃገርካ፡ ከይርኤኻ

ኣብ ገበላ ዓዲቦኻ ኩይንካ ኣወል ቡን ከይሰተኻ

ዋእ፡- ኣይግድን፡ ሕሰበሉ ዳእ። ዓገብ "ኪኒ" (ኢዮ)።

ንምንጃኑ፡ ናበይ ኢኻ ተረቢጽካ ተሃንጢኻ፤

እዛ ዓለም ከንቱ ድያ፡ ጠሊማትካ ከም ኣመላ

ኣርኪባትልካዶ እዛ ጕሓላ

ኣብ ዝወዓለትሉ፡ ዘይትሓድር ከም ዕዋላ

ዘይትርብርብ፡ ጥሓላ፡ ምሒላ

ከንደይ ስድራቤታት፡ ኣጽኒታ ኣጒሳቝላ።

በል ኣንታ፡ ለባምን፡ መስተውዓልን፡ ሓውና

እንካብ ክድካ ከይተሰናበትካና

ንስድራ ቤትካን፡ ፈተውትኻን ጽንዓት ይሃበና

ንዓኻ ኸኣ መንግስተ፡ ሰማያት፡ የውርስልናን፡ ኣሜን።

ዶር ጠዓመ መብራህቱ ብስም ኩሎም ፈተውትኻ ኣብ ሃገረ ብሪጣንያ

(ብሪስቶል ፱፭።፲።፪፻፮ ብዕለት ፲።፮፭።፪፻ ተጻሒፉ፡ ዳሕራይ ዝተጻፈፈ)

Dr Teame Mebrahtu is a former lecturer in Education and an author.

Chapter One

## *'This is why I am here, to help my people'*

### Berhane's service in the Mediterranean, 2017

In 2017, in response to the crisis of refugees crossing the Mediterranean in small boats to reach Europe, Berhane gave up his work as a sessional lecturer at SOAS (School of Oriental and African Studies) and left his busy life in London to take on the role of cultural mediator for Save the Children.

For this role, aged 70, he trained at Dover in marine firefighting and learnt to roll off rafts into the sea. He made two tours in the Mediterranean on the SS Vos Hestia and was involved in the rescue of hundreds of refugees who were moved from small craft on the sea and transported to safety in Sicily.

Following Berhane's death, Gillian Moyes, Save the Children Team Leader on the Vos Hestia, posted this tribute on Facebook (20 November 2020):

### Gillian Moyes

The Save the Children Search & Rescue team and the crew of the Vos Hestia would like to share our deepest condolences with Berhane Woldegabriel's family and many friends. We were shocked and so sad to hear of his passing. Berhane was a unique and highly valued member of our team in 2017, rescuing people attempting the treacherous journey across the Mediterranean Sea in unseaworthy boats.

Berhane's role was as a cultural mediator – he would go out in the rescue dinghy to make first contact with the boats and assure the terrified occupants they were now safe. Once on board ship he used his language skills in Arabic and Tigrinya to support the medical team and protection experts to deal with critical cases. Many rescued people had been through unimaginable horrors, both in their countries of origin and on their journeys. He looked after their needs, listened to them, reassured them.

Berhane was by far the oldest member of our team, but he left most of us for dust when it came to energy! He kept fit by doing step-ups and pull-ups on deck and he was always willing to take the least popular 2am to 4am watch. When we had our first big rescue of people from Eritrea and Ethiopia he came into his own: 'This is why I am here, to help my people'. Berhane was warm, wise, and patient, a true gentleman. His humble demeanour betrayed his incredible life experience and achievements which emerged as he shared stories of his life with us. He was also a lot of fun and was not fazed at all to be hanging out with people less than half his age!

It may have been a small slice of his remarkable life, but Berhane's few months on board the Vos Hestia impacted many people including us, his teammates. We were truly privileged to know him. Rest in peace our dear Berhane.

Two other team mates on the SS Vos Hestia have shared their recollections of Berhane. Dimi Tomova is a nurse who has served on many Search and Rescue missions:

## Dimi Tomova

I met Berhane in Catania at a casual meal for the team about two months before the expeditions. He arrived late and sat opposite me. I was very impressed that he decided to participate at 70. He was very enthusiastic, full of boyish energy. We found that we had the same Eastern Orthodox religion – he was only eating vegetables as he was fasting. We liked each other instantly.

On the missions, he did just about anything, as we all did. As well as his translation role, he helped me in the clinic. Sometimes when we had an influx of refugees, he would go amongst them, organise them and find out what they needed. He loved that and helping in the clinic.

He had this really relaxed laid back attitude. Some of my colleagues didn't like that as there was often a frantic pace going on. He was very efficient, nevertheless. He was respected by the team. He would go by himself and take his laptop, sitting quietly in the corner.

We had some really hard rescues, heart-breaking. He wasn't afraid of anything, pushing his limits. He was bold and experienced. We had great times. You have intense friendships on a mission. We had no opportunity to meet afterwards although we meant to. We used to chat on WhatsApp. I heard from Gillian that he had died. Because I couldn't say goodbye to him, I wrote to him on WhatsApp.

Louis Leeson, who joined the rescue ship as a photographer, recalls that on one such rescue, there were 800 refugees to bring to safety, and it took about twelve hours. On another, tragically, as he relates, the inflatable collapsed before the rescue party could save all those on board, and many drowned. The final act of the rescue divers from the Vos Hestia on each occasion was to sink the emptied inflatable boat that carried the refugees, or what remained of it, so that it could not be used again.

## Louis Leeson

We first met when I came aboard the Vos Hestia in May or June 2017. I thought it was striking that somebody who would have been quite an old man at that point would undertake very physically and emotionally demanding work. I found that to be quite brave.

3

His background as a SOAS lecturer also struck me. SOAS has the reputation of being quite radical and progressive, with left-wing politics. But to see somebody actually go and do something very real and very physical and really make a difference in a practical way was impressive.

He also had a very good sense of humour. He had a sort of slow and ponderous way of talking. You'd ask him a question, and he'd think about it before answering. He might not make the most contributions in a group setting, but when he does, he's making a point.

I remember he never liked to miss breakfast, so he was always up on time for that, but he was never quite as punctual for our 8.30 morning meetings. It became a bit of a running joke... We'd wake up and the first thing he'd ask me is, 'Louis, what time is that meeting that we have?' I was like, 'Berhane, it's 8.30, you know it's 8.30. We do it every day.'

While we were aboard together, we conducted two rescues. In the first there were a lot of Eritreans on board. I think there were upwards of 800 people that they pulled out of the sea, and I photographed them doing that. The operation took around 12 hours. Thankfully, on that one, everyone survived. I think the limit on our boat was much less than 800.

Often, as in the second rescue, the women and children would be in the centre of the boat, and the men would be towards the edge of the boats or even sitting on the side. Tragically, what would happen is the wood in the centre would snap and the men on the side would fall into the water, and it created almost a watery tomb, for want of a better word. Unfortunately, a lot of people did drown, and I saw Berhane going out on those rescue boats.

On board for each rescue there would be a rescue swimmer and a boat man. They would have an Italian translator and an

Arabic translator. And then, you would have Berhane who could speak Tigrinya for the Eritreans.[1] I saw him many times go out onto the rescue boats and reassure people first. The rescue boat doesn't come alongside straight away because then you get a panic, a scramble, people try to jump straight in – so they hold back about 20 metres, speaking English, Tigrinya, Arabic by megaphone, saying 'Please be calm, one by one, children first, then the women, then the men, and we'll take you back to the vessel'. I witnessed him doing that many times. Then dealing with the aftercare.

So you're collecting these people, often roughly 20 kilometres from the Libyan coast, and it's a good 48 hours back to Italy. Along the way, you're having to keep people calm, who've obviously been through some of the most stressful things you could imagine. Some of them crossed Libya and ISIS occupied areas.

Lots of stories were told of people being sold into slavery or held for ransom until their families pay. Often this will be the second or third time that this has happened to them. For some, the journey to get onto that ship could be a year, or two or even three. They could have been detained by multiple different groups, armed militias, robbers, all the way.

It's a very difficult job keeping all those people from different communities in a small compact space, calm, fed and reassured. Even I was roped into this, although I was there as a photographer and journalist. But you can't really afford to have somebody on board and not have a function. So I would also do these patrols at night.

You do three hours just walking amongst people and making sure they're okay and asleep, and if they've got any needs, to go and get help. Obviously Berhane was doing so much more than

---

[1] Berhane was fluent in Tigrinya, Amharic, Arabic and English

I was doing, and he was doing it for many weeks. And he did it very calmly. I don't think I ever really saw him get stressed or angry.

Some of the people who died could have been saved if we'd had more medical staff on board. But on each rotation, there was only one doctor and one nurse. Some of the people coming on board were already dying. Their lungs were filled with water. The nurse, who I worked with very closely, had to triage them as they were coming in. If there had been only one person there, we could have saved this person. But in fact there were 800. You've got to prioritise who can you save and who you cannot. So there were some very hard decisions being made there.

I don't know how much the gory details matter, but there were lots of people who were not at risk of dying but did have very severe burns from the kerosene that fuels the refugee boats. When it mixes with saltwater, it's corrosive to human skin. It burns you. So there were people coming on board with very serious burns. There were people coming in who were incredibly dehydrated because of the scorching hot weather at that time of year, the sun reflecting off the sea. You had lots of pregnant women, women with very small children.

It was a very, very difficult situation that we were all working in, and Berhane was working very hard, because there were so many Tigrinya speakers and I believe he was the only one to speak that language when I was there. I think he was the only person on board that had that breadth of skill. We had an Irish-Sudanese nurse who spoke Arabic, but when it came to the Eritrean and Ethiopian languages, it all fell to him. That's my recollection from being on board the ship with him.

Once everybody was rescued, the rescue divers, who were often ex-military, would slash the boat so it couldn't be reused. You can go on what is effectively the Chinese version of

Amazon to buy these boats. These people smugglers are spending $100 putting 150 people on each one of these things – and charging them thousands. The profits they're making are huge and we simply have no idea how many people drown on that crossing. They'll often be launched from the Libyan coast in threes and fours. They will put an engine on the back with just enough fuel to get them out into international waters, out of Libyan national waters, which I think is 12 kilometres. Also almost every single one of the people I interviewed, believed that you could cross the Mediterranean in a few hours.

I was on board for three weeks and we conducted two rescues that would have rescued upwards of 1100 people. There were some moments of real joy there. We were able to reunite a mother and daughter who had been separated as they'd both gotten on different boats. I think the mother was on one of the rescues that we did, and she was able to tell us, 'My daughter is over there', and we were able to find her. It's one of those really powerful sorts of moments. Other memories leave you with very traumatic stuff that stays with you. Then you also have some very uplifting moments, memories, friendships. A lot of these people were all strangers to me when I got on board. And there are still people, some of whom are some of my closest friends. So it's a bizarre set of circumstances.

*About a year later Louis was with a friend in a bar in Brixton...*

I absentmindedly looked out the window and I see Berhane dressed very dapper, wearing, I think, a cream sort of suit with a matching trilby hat. He was with two or three other gentlemen of a similar age, all of whom were dressed fantastically. I apologised to my friend, and I quickly jumped onto the street and was like, 'Berhane, finally meeting in Brixton!' We had a laugh and a joke. He introduced me to his friends. I forget their names now, but I believe they were Eritrean as well. So he had a little community going on. And that was the last time I saw him... It was very nice, very touching to meet spontaneously and without trying, to just bump into him on home territory.

I'm ashamed to say I didn't have a camera with me because it would have been a very nice photo, these four dapper looking chaps in that quite iconic part of Brixton as well.

During Berhane's service, the rescue boats were already being criticised for contributing to the crisis in the Mediterranean by encouraging migrants to undertake a dangerous journey in the knowledge that if their boats capsized, they would be saved. His belief was that the humanitarian cause of saving lives was of the greatest importance. In the absence of safe routes of entry to the UK and other countries, the people traders flourished, and do still.

*Chapter editor: Amanda Woolley*

Berhane on SS Vos Hestia, on lookout in the Mediterranean

Berhane and fellow trainees, Save the Children

Berhane climbing Mount Etna with the SS Vos Hestia crew, 2017

Berhane and a colleague on board SS Vos Hestia

Berhane in fire-fighting kit, SS Vos Hestia

Berhane and Dimi on board SS Vos Hestia

# 'My dear sole childhood friend and brother...'

## Berhane's life from birth in Eritrea to leaving Ethiopia to Sudan as a refugee (1946-1975)

A combination of recollections from Dr Solomon Ghebre-Ghiorghis, from Berhane himself as recounted to Amanda Woolley[2], and from Haimanot Woldegabriel, Berhane's younger sister.

### Solomon

> My dear sole childhood friend and brother, Berhane Woldegabriel (MA, BA), has sadly passed. But, what an interesting life! In what follows, I will try to provide a short account of Berhane's early life in Asmara in such a way that it will hopefully reflect a slice of the social history of Eritrea in the late 1950s and early 1960s.

> The time was the post-war era and the British Administration of Eritrea had just ended. The Eritrean economy was in shambles and there was a lot of political uncertainty, instability and insecurity since the time of the British.

> To counter the unrest, the British Administration had established a police contingent called the Field Force stationed in a camp in Sembel, which was an old Italian military hospital. That is where Berhane and I met as children because our

---

[2] Berhane spoke of these things over the years. Based on this, Amanda wrote these recollections, and checked this text with Berhane in December 2019.

fathers were members of the said force. We were thus *Deki Sembel* (children from Sembel).

## Amanda

Berhane was born in 1946 on the Orthodox Christmas day (*Ldet*), in the village of Adi Chegnow in Kohain. He was the second child and first son of Woldegabriel Woldegiorgis and Tebereh Adhae. Djazmatch Khassai of Kohain was his father's uncle. Berhane had six sisters and two brothers who survived infancy[3]. These included two half-siblings. He believed that at least three little sisters died as babies.

His parents moved to Asmara in Eritrea when he was very small. At that time, his father, who was born in Tigray, and was formerly a soldier (askari) in the Italian army, had been unjustly accused of murder in his home village, and escaped for his life to become a bandit (*shifta*) in the border country. In the late 1940s, during the British Administration period in Eritrea (1941-52), an amnesty was offered to the *shiftas*, and Berhane's father accepted it, and joined the British police force.

Woldegabriel was promoted to sergeant in Kohain on the border with Tigray, and acquired a reputation for fearlessness and a sense of justice. He became known as *Halow Wossen* which means 'border guard'.

## Solomon

Berhane was quite often known as *Wedi* (son of) *Halow Wossen*. But, he doesn't seem to have liked it. Instead, he preferred to be called *Wedi* (son of) *Wolde*.

---

[3] The children were Askale, Berhane, Tshainesh, Tsblets, Tsegai, Haimanot, Asmelash, Mereb and Kibrom.

**Amanda**

Berhane was raised mostly in the police compound in Sembel, Asmara. Berhane's family was Orthodox Christian, but the community in the police compound was both Christian and Muslim. Berhane grew up seeing no distinction between them, except that his mother told him they were not allowed to eat each other's meat. The football team was run by a Muslim officer, Saleh Bari. Berhane experienced the happiness and freedom to roam that a boy could enjoy in that place and time.

For twelve years, Berhane was the only son, and as such, enjoyed special privileges. He wore a gold earring which he said signified 'favourite child'. He loved his younger sisters dearly but recalled that if he wanted anything, such as warming a cup of milk, they were obliged to serve him. He would fetch and carry foodstuffs, such as oil, for his mother, and run errands, but was not required to do housework.

Once, he was carrying a large containers of oil on his bike, and it fell off and broke. He said that prompted his mother to reproach him as the oil was perhaps a month's supply. This reproach was unusual as he remembered her as unfailingly loving and kind.

The children were more in awe of their father, who was firm but usually fair. Berhane said he only beat him once. The Emperor had recently called for children to concentrate on their education, and Woldegabriel found his son trying to make a radio and apparently neglecting his schoolwork. Berhane felt this beating to be unfair, and thought he should have been commended, not punished.

Despite Woldegabriel's move from *shifta* to policeman, the family remained under the shadow of the blood feud with another family back in the village where he came from. The feud was a particular threat to the lives of Halow Wossen and

Berhane, as the men of the family. Berhane believed that there had been an attempt to poison him when he was a baby in the countryside. He and his father could not return to his father's village, whereas Tebereh and Berhane's sisters could travel to their parents' villages and back in safety. This meant that sometimes Berhane was left with long periods alone with his father, who saw how he missed his mother and teased him for being soft.

Three of Berhane's sisters were sent to Tigray at a young age and had arranged marriages. Berhane's older sister Askale left when he was about seven, and he didn't see her or his younger sister Tsblets again for nearly sixty years, when he was at last able to travel to Tigray. At the time of his visit in (2013) the blood feud was finally laid to rest, and his former opponents admitted that Belamberass[4] Woldegabriel was not guilty of murder.

## Solomon

### Life in the Camp

Early on, our world as children was confined to the camp which was surrounded by a huge wire fence. It was rather suffocating. It was a relief when we reached school age and had to go to Godaif to attend school. Berhane was slightly older than me and one class ahead. All the same, we used to go to school together and became best friends.

After school, we would play football. Quite often, our elders would set us younger boys to fight as a form of entertainment, like the Roman gladiators. It was painful for the children who had to do the fighting because the boys involved became enemies even after the initial fight which continued for quite a long time after that. Interestingly enough, I do not remember any time when Berhane was involved in the fight as an

---

[4] A minor title in Eritrea and Ethiopia at that time

instigator or otherwise. Actually, unlike Berhane, I was one of the notorious fighters, and my nickname was Mussolini, after the Italian dictator.

When there was no school, Berhane, I and our friends would go outside Sembel to far-off places like Arbe Robue, Bizen, Adi Hawsha, Daere Kawlos, Adi Raesi – as far as Shiketi. We visited Arbe Robue a number of times because there was plenty of *beles* (cactus fruit) there. We were shabbily dressed kids, quite often semi-malnourished because of the prevailing poverty of the time. Thus, whenever we visited Arbe Rebue, it was a feast day.

### Collecting firewood, kubo (cow dung) and wild vegetables

Each policeman in the camp was given a one-room accommodation for his family, including that of Berhane and mine. There was one bed for the father, and curiously, another for the mother and a third one for the children (boys and girls). The room also served as a kitchen and living room. The furniture was dire. *Enjera* (bread) was baked outside.

The salary of a police constable was about 30 Birr per month, and that of a sergeant about 40 Birr. There was not enough money to buy firewood. Therefore, we children were expected to collect firewood and cow dung from the fields stretching for a number of kilometres outside the camp. During the rainy season, we were also required to gather vegetables to supplement the family's meagre food supply.

All the same, we did not consider ourselves particularly impoverished. Almost everybody was poor, and we did not particularly feel the pain. There were many Eritreans in worse position during that time.

## School

All school-age children in the camp were enrolled at Godaif Elementary and Middle School. The school was about 2-3 kilometres from our camp. Due to the scarcity of seats in each class, students were placed either in the morning or afternoon shift. We were provided with one cup of milk by UNICEF five days a week. The school had only one rusty water tank which was intermittently filled. Most of the days, there was no drop of water in the school. There was no proper toilet arrangement in the school either. We sometimes had to go from house to house in the village begging for water.

Berhane was a good student, and he had no problem passing from grade to grade, whereas I had a dodgy academic record because I didn't care about school. Our parents did not go to school, and our mothers could not read and write, although our fathers could. There was no facility at home for children who wanted to study. After school, we would quickly put aside our exercise books (we never had any books at all) and go out to play with our mates. During exam time, we did the revision on our way to school on the very day of the exam. Nobody supervised us at least until we finished 5th grade.

## Playing truant

One day, we were bored of school, and Berhane, me and Tesfalidet decided to abscond from class and go to Kombishtato, Asmara city centre to have a wild day of drama. Our main target was the Italian shops in the main street full of mirrors, toys of Habesha[5] women, men and children clad in traditional clothes, nice dresses, horse meat, flowers, modern furniture, ice cream, etc. It was like visiting Europe itself,

---

[5] Habesha, term used to identity the people lived primarily in the Abyssinian Plateau which covers the highlands of Eritrea and Ethiopia

especially Italy. The shopkeepers were almost invariably Italian, and they were saying *Bon giorno, Bona siera,* etc.

We were particularly fascinated by the mirrors which reflected our images. We had no mirrors at home. We would check our images in the mirror every time we visited a shop and compared it to the previous image – and have a good laugh. We were in a different world and level of existence – and nobody remembered the school we had fled from.

Obviously, we left home with our exercise books. But there was no way that we would go to Kombishtato with our school gear on. We had to hide the stuff in a stone quarry behind a hill on the way to school. After the treat we had in Kombishtato, we had to think about how we could retrieve our stuff in time and rejoin the school children returning from school. We decided that we would reach the hiding place in time and wait there until some of the returning students had gone past our hiding place. We thus managed to join the crowd of returning students without being noticed.

## The only radio receiver in the camp

There was only one radio receiver in the camp in 1960, to be precise. That is the year when General Mengistu Niway and Girmamiye Neway rebelled against the Haile Selassie regime and many officials were killed. I remember the occasion as if it was yesterday. Berhane and I and many of the residents of the camp sat outside the house where the radio was. The program was in Amharic, and Berhane and I did not understand Amharic, but some people were providing us with a rough translation. Anyway, we were not there for the news but for the music.

## Amanda

### Berhane at Comboni School, Asmara

For a few years until he was twelve, Berhane had a private education at the Catholic Comboni School in Asmara. Other pupils included the children of Italian fathers and Eritrean mothers. Although he made friends, Berhane felt out of place, as many of his classmates were from wealthy families. He said they wore wool while he wore cotton. Many brought sandwiches for lunch, while he had home-made *injera*.[6] Berhane appreciated that he had a good education at Comboni, but was relieved when his father removed him.

## Solomon

### Gaining access to the cinema

Comboni School students were given the privilege of watching the cinema on the school premises once a week. Watching the cinema was new to us, and we would hear the stories Berhane told us about what he saw with our mouths open. There was a film called Mother India. There was also Bonanza and Ben Hur. From what we heard, we would do anything to gain access to the cinema even though we were not Comboni students.

If a Comboni student wanted to enter the cinema, either his class monitor had to confirm that he was indeed a Comboni student, or the student had to pass certain security questions. That is where Berhane was of great help. He would tell us what to say: which grade, which class, location of the class, name of the class teacher, his appearance, some names of the classmates and other teachers. We were so desperate to get in that we carefully studied all the details before presenting ourselves at the gate. Sometimes, we succeeded in gaining access. Other

---

[6] A sour fermented flatbread, like a pancake which is a staple food in Eritrea, Ethiopia and parts of Sudan

times, we were caught. All the same, it was worth the effort. Thanks to Berheen[7]!

### Discovering backyard access to Cinema Asmara

As children of policemen, we did not even have enough to eat, let alone pay to attend a performance of *Mahber Tiatr Asmera* (Asmara Theatre Club) at Cinema Asmara. But we were desperate to gain access and watch the legendary figures of the time perform. We were boys from the outskirts of the city, and we were not familiar with what was possible and was not. Berhane, who was more mature and well-connected than most of us, told us that there was a boy who could help us climb a wall in the backyard of the building that could lead us to a second-floor window which was usually left open.

We waited outside the theatre until about 30 minutes had elapsed since the play started. Luckily, the guards and usherers had left the entrance open as they went inside to watch the play themselves. Thus, we quickly sneaked into the backyard with the help of our guide. Lo and behold, in one corner of the building, there were protruding carved stones spaced about 20 centimetres apart. We went up the wall without difficulty and jumped onto the balcony. We hid there for a while and checked the windows one by one. Two of them were open, and we quietly jumped in and dispersed. We could not get seats – but that was fine.

It was amazing. There was Tiberh Tesfahunegn singing *Defar Gasha, Memhir Alemayehu Wetru Higus* performing a comical song *Seatey Tesera*, and Alamin Abdel Letif singing *Dehan Kuni Aba Shawl!*. After that treat, we would not have cared if we had been caught and condemned to a firing squad.

---

[7] Diminutive of Berhane

## American rubbish dump

Other unusual exploits led by Berhane were our frequent visits to the American rubbish dump at *Cambo Bolo*, near the Asmara Expo. Surprisingly, despite our poverty, our aim was not to find something to sell – we were too proud for that. We were looking for unusual metals – wires, batteries, discarded remains of radio sets, crystals, etc. The aim was to assemble a radio set. We did a lot of experiments with wires and crystals. We also secured some speakers. In the end, nothing came out of our experimentation, and we abandoned the idea. But our attempt to create a telephone system over almost a quarter of a kilometre or so did succeed. It was a consolation of sorts. Anyway, the audacious plan of assembling a radio receiver from discarded wires and metals at that time was amazing.

## First experience of corruption

Upon the suggestion of Berhane, a group of us children decided to go from house to house with a *Hiya Hoye* (burning torch) in our hands to wish every family in the neighbourhood *Kidus Yohannes* (Happy New Year). Traditionally, the families were supposed to give money to the young well-wishers.

There was a bigger boy among us who volunteered to act as a cashier for the group. A fair amount of money was collected, and we were all expecting to get a share of it. Since it was getting late at night, we decided that we would meet the next morning to decide how to share the collection. At 10am, we came to the meeting place as agreed, but the cashier had disappeared. However, he sent someone to let us know that he had lost the money but did not know where or how. We were bewildered, and we did not know what to do.

I remember it as if it happened yesterday. The big boy robbing innocent young children of their hard-earned money in this way was a terrible crime. Berhane in his usual generous spirit might have said let bygones be bygones, and forgotten it altogether. On my part, I can neither forget nor forgive!

## Berhane in high school

After Berhane had attended Comboni School for a few years, his family was transferred to Mendefera, where he attended the famous St George's School.[8]

Berhane and I then joined Prince Makonnen Secondary School in Asmara together in grade nine in the early 1960s, and he never returned to Sembel. His parents were then in Mendefera, and he had to rent a house in Asmara with his mates. Students living on their own had wider experiences which allowed them to build a vast network of friends, acquaintances and political activists in Asmara. Berhane even started to participate in political meetings with people like Isaias Afwerki, Zewengiel etc. who later became important personalities in Eritrean politics.

## Amanda

Every day, his mother would send *injera* with the driver of the bus that ran between Mendefera and Asmara, and Berhane would meet the bus and collect his dinner. He said that he was very preoccupied with his school and social life, and on occasion would forget to meet the bus! His poor mother would have the meal returned to her later by the driver.

Berhane excelled at school, and in his late teens was one of the top 200 students in Eritrea and Ethiopia in his exams. His father was informed of this via the police radio. Berhane opted

---

8 One of the most vivid memories of Berhane's younger sister, Haimanot, was of him playing the General Brambori for the school drama.

to be a teacher, against his father's wishes. His father would have liked him to be a lawyer.

Berhane went for training, to Debre Bihan Teacher Training Institute, Ethiopia, from 1965-7 and received his Teaching Diploma. In 1969 he enrolled in Haile Selassie University, Addis Ababa, and he was awarded a BA degree in History in 1973.

A CV that he wrote in 2019 records that between 1967 and 1975 he was a teacher in various public and private schools in Ethiopia, Eritrea and Sudan. This included about two years in Shawa Gimira, Kaffa, which he had to leave because of severe asthma. During that period, Haimanot remembers Berhane visiting the family in Asmara and bringing traditional dresses.

In 1973, he taught Amharic and 'cross-culture' to the US Peace Corps in Awasa. The following year, Berhane taught for a year in Agordat, in order to get to know the Eritrean lowlands. It was part of his University Mandatory National Service Programme. This was an opportunity for his sister Haimanot to have a free high school education, and Berhane took her with him, in what proved to be a successful arrangement.

## Haimanot

I got to know Berhane very well when he took me to Agordat to live and study with him. As I was a student at the school where he was teaching, we used to walk together along the rail track to school and back. As a result, some of the students and teachers joked that we needed to follow the rail track so as not to get lost on our way home!

It was the mid-'70s when there was a lot of talk about *Tegadelti* (freedom fighters), especially the ELF (Eritrean Liberation Front) who were moving around Agordat. Berhane was very protective of me not to get influenced and always discouraged me from discussing it, telling me, 'Please concentrate on your studies'. However, he used to sneak out at night and meet with *Tegadelti*. I knew he was meeting them, but I didn't mention it to him at the time due to fear of upsetting him. Later on, he told me that he used to meet Said Saleh.

## Amanda

During Berhane's time at Haile Selassie University, Ethiopia was in ferment. The Emperor, who had won international respect for his dignity in exile in the 1930s, and for his subsequent roles in the Pan-African Congress and the UN was by then considered reactionary in domestic politics.

As a student, Berhane was involved in demonstrations against the imperial regime, and remembered being selected to carry a banner because he had a smart jacket. These demonstrations came under fire, and some of his comrades died.

In 1975, Berhane went as a Field Officer for the Christian Relief Association, Wollo. By this time, he was married to Abinet and had a young son, Yemane. The increasing power of Mengistu's regime led to the Red Terror, and Berhane had to flee to Sudan on foot, leaving his family behind. He crossed the crocodile-infested River Akobo, from western Ethiopia into Sudan (now South Sudan), then made the long journey up to Port Sudan, passing through the Nile Valley electricity headquarters en route.

*Chapter editor: Peter Riddell*

Berhane's teacher's ID (AW)

Berhane with a friend and
colleague, Shawa Gimira

Berhane with a group,
Shawa Gimira

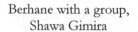

Berhane and colleagues, Ethiopia

Berhane, teacher, in Shawa Gimira, Kaffa, Ethiopia

Berhane, teacher, in Shawa Gimira, Kaffa

Berhane as a student

Berhane
with
students
and
colleagues,
Shawa
Gimira

Berhane riding with colleagues and others, Shawa Gimira

Berhane with
colleagues, Shawa
Gimira

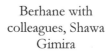

...and children.

Chapter Three
# 'Berhane Sudanow'

## Berhane's life in Sudan 1975-1990

### Haimanot, Berhane's sister, remembers:

*Compared to my other brothers and sisters I am the lucky one who got the chance to spend more time with Berhane. First I spent a year with him in Agordat and then we met again in Sudan when I immigrated. He was well connected in Sudan and whenever I needed help, he was there for me.*

*Sometimes he had very expensive jokes. One time I had a celebration at home, and I brewed siwa (traditional beer). He came to visit me and when he tasted the drink, he was making fun of it saying, 'It is not as good as mum's but as the brother I have no choice but to drink it.' I thought he was serious and was very cross with him but didn't say anything.*

*When he left I was still very upset, and my husband asked me why I am upset, and I told him because of what Berhane said about my siwa and then Gezae (my husband) started to laugh that I didn't know Berhane was joking. From that time on I got used to his expensive jokes.*

Berhane arrived in Sudan in 1975 as a refugee with nothing. He became a teacher at the Comboni School, Port Sudan. Here he was popular, particularly with the Eritrean boys. One day, he was late, because he had washed his only pair of trousers and had to wait for them to dry. When the boys learnt of this, they brought him in extra clothes from home.[9] After teaching for a year in the Comboni School, he forged a distinguished career in journalism before having to leave the country in 1990.

---

[9] Berhane related this to Amanda Woolley

During these years, Sudan accepted thousands of refugees from other African countries and accommodated the majority in camps. The largest numbers came from Eritrea and Ethiopia, but there were also many from Uganda, Chad and Zaire. In his capacity as Reporter, then Senior Reporter for Sudanow, Berhane wrote extensively on refugee and development issues and on the situation in Eritrea, becoming known as 'Berhane Sudanow'. Berhane focused several articles on the plight of the Eritreans in refugee camps.[10]

Berhane worked with aid agencies on the ground in Sudan and became allied in work and friendship with the late Dr Ahmed Karadawi of the UN High Commission for Refugees, which sought to better the condition of refugees, in Sudan and throughout Africa, by improving their basic services and human rights.

While in Sudan, Berhane attained degrees from the University of Khartoum, a BSc in Economics and Politics (1978-81) and an MSc in Development Studies (1989-90). He also continued his original vocation as a teacher, this time for the Sudan Council of Churches, as a part-time trainer in English and Cross-Culture, preparing refugees for resettlement in the USA and EU.

After working as head of a German Vocational Training Project in Kassala (GTZ[11]), he spent his last three years in Sudan as Head of Information for the Refugees Administration in the Ministry of the Interior, based in Showak. While he was there, the democratically elected government of Sadiq-el-Mahdi was overthrown by the coup of Omar Al-Bashir. In 1992, Berhane was threatened with arrest because of an article he wrote on food

---

[10] See Appendix (articles by Berhane in Sudanow)
[11] German government-owned corporation for international cooperation with world-wide operations

distribution, and he fled as a refugee to the UK. He left without fulfilling his hope of publishing his own magazine.

During his time in Sudan, Berhane met and married his second wife, Azeib, with whom he had two children, Medhanie and Fewien.

The following accounts from Berhane's friends and colleagues indicate the scope of his activities in Sudan and his continued engagement with Eritrean politics and with the enduring plight of its refugees.

Mohamed Kheir Omer, who worked as a veterinary surgeon was a close associate and friend throughout Berhane's time in Sudan. His obituary is a fitting introduction to the recollections in this chapter of Berhane's life.

## Berhane Woldegabriel: 'A noble universal human being'
**Mohamed Kheir Omer**

I knew Berhane for almost the last 50 years, and we have been very close. We regarded each more as brothers than friends. I knew his family as he knew mine. We knew the details of those we were not lucky enough to meet. If there was a Muslim holiday, I was the first to wish him a nice one and vice versa.

The first time I knew him was when he was assigned as a national service student from Addis Ababa University to Agordat. I think it was his choice to come to Agordat. I was a 1st-year student, and he was a 3rd-year student. He used to have contacts with the ELF when he was there.

I moved to Sudan in 1975 as a student at Khartoum University, and he followed suit a couple of years later, and our relations consolidated. I joined the Sudan Commission for Refugees (COR) in 1982, and he joined COR a few years later. We were based in Showak, and we were the only refugees who were department heads in COR. I was head of the Veterinary and Animal Production Department, and he was the Head of a newly established Department of Communications. Previously he had lived in Khartoum and worked for Sudanow. He wrote many interesting articles, some of which were investigative, and became a famous journalist. We worked for the cause of Eritrean refugees in Sudan.

In Khartoum, Berhane was a member of the EPLF (Eritrean People's Liberation Front), to begin with. In one of the meetings, a cadre stated that EPLF had ideological differences with the ELF. Berhane challenged the cadre that there were none. The cadre angrily told him, 'Wuzaa' ('Get out, get lost'). That was his last time with the EPLF.

We had two big dreams that were not materialised: writing a children's book with illustrations in local Eritrean languages, and a non-political magazine that addressed social issues that face refugees.

There is a story about publishing the magazine. A friend of Berhane's in the EPLF arranged for him to meet Isaias Afwerki[12] in the field. During his stay, he met Isaias, who proposed that the EPLF could fund the publication. Knowing that Berhane was a famous journalist in Sudan, the EPLF wanted to win him over. Berhane did not accept the offer as he knew it would not be neutral if funded by the organisation. After many efforts, Berhane secured permission from the press and publications' commission to publish the magazine.

On June 29, 1989, we stayed late at night to review the first issue in his office and went to bed late. I woke up early in the morning, and when I opened the radio, there was just military

---

[12] Eritrean People's Liberation Front Secretary General, President from 24 May 1993

march music, which was an indication of a coup. Later came the first proclamation of the Omar Al-Bashir coup. It was a sad day, and there was no way we could publish the magazine afterwards. A few months later, Berhane was tipped off by a friend that the Islamist government was planning to arrest him, and he had to leave Sudan at short notice for the UK.

I used to meet him whenever I visited London, and he once called on me in Oslo. I very much enjoyed his company and the intellectual discussions we had. He used to take me to his Sudanese friends, who respected him very much. But he had friends of different nationalities, Ethiopians, other Africans, Arabs, Jews, British and others, and in all walks of life. London will be empty without him.

As a person, Berhane was kind, generous, caring, considerate, trustworthy, and accepting of others as they were. He was firm in his beliefs but non-confrontational. If he disagreed, he did so with respect. He worked hard to bring Eritreans of different ethnic, religious, and political backgrounds together.

His last project was to get the leaders of all the Eritrean political organisations together. The meeting was due to take place in London in March 2020, and he asked me to chair it. At the last minute, the meeting was cancelled due to the introduction of anti-Covid 19 measures.

Among other roles, he was a founder-member of the Board of Trustees of the EEPT (Eritrean Education and Publication Trust). He also taught Tigrinya Teacher at London University's School of Oriental and Africa Studies (SOAS) from September 2008. He was an experienced educator with broad experience in non-profit organisations, intercultural communication, policy analysis, translation, and lecturing. He studied at the universities of Addis Ababa, Khartoum, and Leeds. He also worked for Search and Rescue Operations in the Mediterranean before its closure.

He will be deeply missed – but I live with the pleasant memories I had of him over five decades. May his soul rest in peace – my condolences to his children, his brother and sisters, and all family and friends.

## Ghirmai Negash

I met Berhane first in Khartoum when he was working for Sudanow. Although we had only just met and I didn't have any previous experience with publishing in English, he kindly hired me as his assistant on some of the articles he was writing.

One project we worked on together that stands out was about refugees in Sudan. The focus was on the criteria and procedures used to choose who would qualify for the UN-sponsored programs for refugees to resettle in a third country. The job didn't pay much, but I cherished the opportunity to work with Berhane and learn from the experience.

I met Berhane twice after this project, in Amsterdam and in Sheffield. On both occasions, we reminisced about life in Sudan and also talked about the idea of launching an independent newspaper in the Diaspora. As he explained it, it was going to be similar to the journal Mohammed Kheir referred to in his tribute. Berhane was remarkably consistent, even obsessive, in his ideas.

As a person, Berhane was a good-natured and passionate individual, who, indiscriminately, cared much about all refugee communities in Khartoum. Many who knew him from those days have very fond memories of his forthcoming, compassionate, loving, and outgoing personality. Above all though, he was a doer and a dreamer. Like all doers and dreamers, he achieved some, failed in some, and sadly left with more to dream and do.'

May his soul rest in perfect peace!

## Petros Tesfagiorgis

I met the late Berhane Woldegabriel for the first time in the early '80s in a conference on Eritrean refugees in Sudan at St Anne's College, Oxford University, at which I represented the Eritrean Relief Association in the UK. The conference was organised by Dr Barbara Harrell-Bond, an anthropologist who later founded the Oxford University Refugee Studies Centre. At that time Berhane was a journalist with Sudanow.

The conference was to address the inadequacy of the services given to Eritrean refugees in the refugee camps in Sudan. The presence of Dr. Ahmed Karadawi, Sudanese commissioner of refugees, suggested that the Sudanese government was ready to accept recommendations of measures that would improve the refugees' lives.

Berhane introduced me to the commissioner, and we had a long discussion about the living conditions of the refugees. Berhane believed that the service given to the Eritrean refugees were not enough. He was continuously in touch with the refugees and listened to their grievances and passed them to the commissioner and other Sudanese authorities. He became the voice of the refugees by expressing parents' concern that their children were not getting enough food to sustain them, and that the health service was inadequate. The parents wanted their children to have a modern education in order to get professional jobs when they finished their studies. He tried his best to convince the participants of the conference of the need of more support to the refugees.

At a time when Eritrean girls were married at a young age, and then were meant to stay at home to look after the children, do the cooking and washing, and serve their husbands, Berhane's advice to parents was to give girls equal opportunities to the boys and to enrol them in schools.

37

## Yacoub Idris

Our beloved and forever missed brother, the late Berhane Woldegabriel and I met in Khartoum in the second half of 1982 when I joined Khartoum University for an MA Degree. Berhane, the ever smiling and funny fellow, was a bundle of joy to be around. At the time was known as 'Berhane Sudanow' due to his association with Sudanow.

In April 1984, when I worked for the Sudanese Commissioner Office for Refugees in Eastern Sudan, we were part of a group which attended the symposium on African Refugees at St Anne's College, Oxford University (mentioned by Petros Tesfagiorgis above).

Once back in Sudan, Berhane and I were hired by Dr Schoenmeir of the Saar Institute of Psychology, as research associates and we lived in the guest house of the town of Khashm Elgirba in Eastern Sudan. We had two of the best weeks of my life filled with lots of fun. That was the time when we got to know each other better.

In Khartoum, I remember meeting Berhane at the Sudan Council of Churches where he was on the Education Council.

In the late 1980s, Berhane and I met several times and spent good times socialising and talking about various topics in the refugee field. I remember meeting his ex-wife, Azeib, the mother of two of his children, when they came from Germany to visit him in Khartoum. I also remember visiting him at his home with his ex-partner Jennie Street.

After I left Sudan for Canada, we were completely disconnected until not long before he passed away.

Berhane was a man of great initiative who worked relentlessly to see his community unite and prosper. I am so saddened by his loss. May his soul rest in peace, and heartfelt condolences to his big family and all his friends around the world.

## Christine Brown

I first met Berhane in Sudan in 1987. He was a journalist and a project officer with the Commission for Refugees, based in Showak.[13] I was working for World University Service UK, based in Gedaref. Our paths crossed through our work, and, like many others, I was charmed by him – in fact it wasn't long before I fell in love with him. We became lovers and we would meet whenever our busy work schedules allowed. This continued until my contract ended and I returned to the UK just a few months later.

I met Berhane again a couple of years later when he had fled to the UK. We weren't lovers this time, but we became good friends. We met, not often, but regularly over the years. He developed a loving relationship with my son.

Like most people, there are times when my mind tricks me into believing that I am not good enough or that others don't like me. When I was with him, I always knew that he loved me and admired me as I loved and admired him. His gentle presence brought me peace and reminded me of my own worth. I miss Berhane.

I don't believe I am alone in being reminded of my own worth by Berhane's presence. He brought that same delightful, peaceful awareness to many others whose lives he touched.

## Andy Gregg

I first met Berhane in the early 1990s as he had become a friend of my late father, Dr Ian Gregg. Berhane had met him when

---

[13] Head of Information, Commission for Refugees, Showak, 1987-1990

he was on his way into the liberated areas of Northern Eritrea in 1989 as a visiting doctor who had heard about the successes of the Eritrean public health programmes in those areas. Ian struck up an immediate friendship with Berhane and was able to use his specialist medical knowledge of pulmonary diseases to treat Berhane's recurring asthma.

For many years Berhane was a journalist in Sudan and he always had a substantial knowledge of the politics and culture of the Horn of Africa in general, and Sudan and Eritrea in particular. As a journalist he maintained a strongly independent line and refused to be associated with any particular position or Eritrean front organisation despite being a passionate supporter of the long Eritrean liberation struggle against Ethiopia. This independence was not always welcomed and occasionally meant him facing some personal danger and frequent accusations that he was a spy.

With the coup of Omar Al-Bashir against the democratic Sudanese government, Berhane's settled and fulfilling life in Sudan came to an end. For the second time he became a refugee, this time to the UK where he was to live for the rest of his life.

*Chapter editor, Amanda Woolley.*

Berhane's identity pass, Sudanow (AW)

Berhane with Ahmed Karadawi in Sudan, 1980s (AY)

Berhane in Showak, Sudan (CB)

Berhane (AY)

Chapter Four

## 'London will be empty without him'

### Berhane's life in Sheffield and London 1990-2020

When Berhane arrived in the UK in 1990, it was to attend a conference. After the conference, he decided to leave the UK for the Netherlands and then travel back to Hull[14] on a public ferry, in order that he could claim asylum legally on re-entry.

He first settled in Sheffield, where he held part-time appointments as an Amharic tutor in the University of Sheffield and as a Lecturer in Media Studies at Royal Hallam University. During this time, his partner was Jennie Street, whom he met when they were both working in Sudan. Their son Hadish was born in 1992.

### London as home

Berhane came to London in late 1992 for work, and it remained his base for the rest of his life. It was the longest he lived continuously in one place. He settled in Lambeth which in the early 1990s had the largest concentration of Eritrean refugees in the country. From 1993-2009 he lived with Amanda Woolley in Kennington.

It was in London that Berhane started the pattern that remained for the rest of his life, combining work with community activity and continuing engagement in the politics of Eritrea, always in the wider context of the Horn of Africa.

---

[14] Port in north-east England

## Working with refugees in the educational and voluntary sectors

Berhane's first job in London was as Manager of the Ethnic Minority Employment and Education Project at Kensington and Chelsea College. Ursula Howard, then College Vice-Principal recalls the impact he made:

### Ursula Howard

I first met Berhane in 1992. He put his head round the door of my office at Kensington and Chelsea College in the World's End area of Chelsea – and asked with a smile if we could talk.

I was the Vice-Principal and he'd been appointed Project Manager for the Managed Ethnic Minority Employment and Education Project, a voluntary scheme to help immigrants and refugees, mainly but not only from African countries, to find work or vocational training.

Berhane's gravitas, charisma and charm worked instantly. Uncharacteristically, I simply stopped what I was doing, sat down there and then, and listened, becoming a bit more like him than the over-busy manager who would normally schedule a meeting later in the week.

Berhane was there to ask me if I could persuade the Principal and fellow College managers to allow the project to move long-term into an empty lodge-house near the college gates.

Berhane's powers of persuasion were not the words he used, but his presence and the respect his seriousness engendered in others. I was soon his advocate, trying to persuade reluctant senior colleagues. There wasn't enough money in the project to make it attractive, income generation was king, and the college was hoping to expand more lucrative courses. And they were resentful of the Local Authority's wish, as the owners of the buildings, to house the refugee project in the college.

Happily, the project stayed there for its lifespan. Berhane made many friends among teaching and support staff, a popular colleague who engendered a spirit of mutual support. It was there that he met his long-term partner Amanda Woolley, who was the college's IT coordinator.

Ever since the early 1980s, any funded learning for people new to the UK – and indeed for working-class unemployed people – was not about what a person wanted to learn, nor did it build on their existing education, their hopes and dreams, their languages, skills or cultures.

On the contrary, starting with the curriculum for ESOL (English for Speakers of Other Languages) or literacy, learning was instrumental: geared to one overriding desired outcome: getting people into work and off benefits as quickly as possible.

The Ethnic Minority project at least had education in the title, rather than simply pre-skills, job skills or training. Taking people and their education seriously was Berhane's approach to adults engaged in learning. He worked with the whole person and their life experiences, which were often tough to the point of persecution, and which he'd known too well himself.

His way was listening, talking, smiling, facilitating communication, taking time with people, encouraging, building confidence and connections. His powers of understanding people, and sharply intelligent analysis of systems and power relationships, cut through muddled thinking into clear light. But he exercised his formidable intellect gently, pushing discussions forward in a positive direction.

Whether helping new asylum seekers as a translator, working as a mediator, or training teachers of adult basic education at the ILEA (Inner London Education Authority) LLU

45

(Language and Literacy Unit)[15], where, in the early 2000s, he was a much-loved colleague whom no-one would have dreamt of trying to channel into government-led models of how teachers should teach.

Berhane was unafraid to speak truth to power, or to tell people who were struggling to find their way, how they might embrace a stronger sense of the realities of the world and so help themselves better. My son was one person he helped to move out of a troubled life because he respected Berhane and felt befriended.

Berhane left Kensington and Chelsea College to take a year's contract with Human Rights Watch Africa in 1994. This included some time in Ethiopia, when he visited Addis Ababa, Shashamane, Dire Dawa and Jimma (where he had taught in the early 70s). Susan Quick, who met him during this trip, recalled that they were held up at gunpoint while returning to Addis Ababa.

In 1996, Berhane started work for GHARWEG (Ghana Refugee & Welfare Group), a project based in Waterloo. He was teaching ESOL, and working with the long-term unemployed, refugees and asylum seekers. He became good friends with his manager, Nyeya Yen. Yen's tribute captures exactly Berhane's engagement with both his work and community activities, which overlapped.

### Nyeya Yen

I do not know how to start paying a tribute to the late Berhane Woldegabriel. Is it the humorous Berhane or the very serious conscientious Berhane or the fighter for social justice for Africa and the world? Or the hard-working English for Speakers of Other Languages Berhane?

---

[15] The LLU later relocated to South Bank University, and had a national scope

I met Berhane in the early '90s. A group of political exiles from Ghana had teamed up with other Africans based in the UK and, together with Africans of diasporic descent, formed ARIB (Africa Research & Information Bureau). We felt that Africa's story must be told by Africans who have connections with the continent and not through the lenses of European Africa experts. As a result, we set up the Africa World Review (AWR), a periodic magazine that was written only by Africans and provided a perspective of Africa from an African viewpoint.

We also set up GHARWEG Advice, Training & Careers Centre providing advice on welfare and benefits to refugees and asylum seekers. Our training section ran a series of courses including teaching ESOL for which Berhane was responsible for six or more years. He helped hundreds of refugees to learn English in order to help them integrate into British society. He was so meticulous and provided excellent monitoring and evaluation reports for the project that we continually secured funding. He had such amazing gifts and made friends with a lot of his trainees.

If there was one thing that our collective missed, it was a perspective from the Horn of Africa. This Berhane also brought, with articles providing an incisive analysis of events in that region, and other writers especially from Eritrea and Ethiopia. This improved the image of AWR as representative of the voice of Pan-Africanism.

Together with Berhane we engaged in the liberation struggles of South Africa and other colonised countries across the world. We took part in demonstrations and sit-ins outside African embassies against military dictatorships and one-party rule.

As an elder brother, he counselled us and shared his experience to guide us in our struggle for social and economic justice. There was hardly any time that I saw Berhane in confrontation or conflict with anybody. When there were stressful situations, he turned heated debates into jokes and toned down tempers. He was always an advisor and counsellor.

As if this was not enough Berhane founded the EEPT (Eritrean Education and Publication Trust), bringing together diverse Eritrean and Ethiopian perspectives in publications, workshops and seminars.

Apart from the above, I have a natural affinity with Berhane. He genuinely treated me like a junior brother. In fact, Berhane treated everybody as an equal with respect and dignity. When I moved back to Ghana, and on my visits to the UK, we would often meet for coffee. We discussed him coming to visit me in Ghana. It was therefore a shock when Berhane passed away without fulfilling that hope.

Africa has lost lots of good, conscientious, and honest people, and Berhane was one of them. Sometimes when I feel lonely and depressed about the state of African countries, I think of people like Berhane who spent their entire lives struggling for economic and social emancipation without seeing it realised. Then I say to myself, 'Well, others have tried. If Berhane has done his bit and not seen the liberation of Africa, you also do yours and hand the baton to others.' I will continue to hold the baton and pass it to the next generation. That is continuing the tradition of Berhane. May the soul of Berhane live forever.

## Working together for Conflict Resolution, Mediation and Peace

Yen refers to the charity Berhane founded in 1995, the EEPT. Berhane remained a trustee of the EEPT for life, influencing and steering its activity. The charity originated, organised, planned, and attended programmes and courses in Conflict Resolution and mediation in partnership with IofC (Initiatives of Change UK).

Berhane became involved with IofC in the late 1990s. He was a regular attender at their weekly AfR (Agenda for Reconciliation)

48

meetings in Victoria and went on several occasions to IofC's international conferences in Caux, Switzerland. Berhane's friend Amanuel Yemane, trustee and treasurer of EEPT, recalls his work in both organisations:

## Amanuel Yemane

Berhane held the jigsaw of Eritrean society together. It is divided by political and cultural issues, and highland and lowland[16]. Because of Berhane's listening skills and his ability to see things from the point of view of the victim or the other, he enabled the EEPT, with the support of the IofC, to undertake reconciliation and education projects amongst the Eritrean community in which he commanded respect from all sides.

Berhane's ability to listen to, to connect and to relate to people enabled him to build a wide network. Among them were Dr Mohamed Suliman (founder member of the Institute for African Alternatives), Sadiq El-Mahdi (former Prime Minister of Sudan), General Burma Nasser (currently acting head of the UMMA party of Sudan), Mama Khadija Hussein (former Culture Minister of Sudan and founder of Mothers for Peace), Ambassador Mohamed Sharif Mohamud from Somalia, and the Hon. Osman Jama Ali (former deputy PM of Somalia and founder and Chairman of the Somali Initiative for Dialogue and Democracy).

Whenever he planned a conference or meeting, people would queue up to attend. This only happened when Berhane was known to be involved.'

---

[16] Referring to the divisions between 'highland' and 'lowland' Eritreans

## Work with refugees and asylum seekers: helping to change UK government policy

In the mid-1990s, Berhane worked with his Sudanese friend, the late Al-Fatah Salman, in the Horn of Africa Federation. They, and their colleagues in the Federation believed that through uniting and burying their differences, the countries of the Horn of Africa could become a strong and effective bloc.

Relations between Ethiopia and Eritrea were initially friendly after Eritrea gained independence in 1993. But within a few years, numbers of Eritrean refugees increased due to growing repression in Eritrea under President Isaias Afwerki, and in particular following the Eritrean-Ethiopian War (1998-2000 also known as the Badme War).

Berhane was heartbroken at the outbreak of the war, not only because it undermined the chance of wider unity, but because of the hostility it caused between Eritreans and Ethiopians in the UK. Due to Berhane's own ancestry in Tigray and Eritrea, he found it hard to bear, and felt a level of ostracism for his own views.

In late 2001, Berhane's friend Petros Tesfagiorgis fled from the growing repression of its citizens by the Eritrean government of Isaias Afwerki.

### Petros Tesfagiorgis

On September 18, 2001, top Eritrean government officials were arrested for calling for the implementation of the constitution and a nationwide election. The prisoners were nicknamed the G-15. It was actually Isaias Afwerki's coup d'état to avoid an election that would give power to the people. At the same time, he imprisoned the editors of the private newspapers and banned freedom of expression. All these repressions gave rise to the exodus of huge numbers of Eritrean citizens.

After the arrest of the G-15 it was obvious that Afwerki would start to arrest those who sympathised with the G-15 and the journalists. I decided to leave the country because there was a reason for the government to go after me.

Since the outbreak of the Ethio-Eritrean war in May 1998, ethnic Eritrean citizens of Ethiopia were being deported to Eritrea at the rate of about 7,000 people per month. After some months the number rose to more than 70,000. I and few friends established an NGO called CPE (Citizens for Peace in Eritrea) in order to document the human rights violations in the process of those deportations. They had left behind everything they had and were destitute. We campaigned that they were entitled to be acknowledged as refugees and should be supported by UNHCR.

In 2001 Semere Kessete, President of the Asmara University Student Union was arrested. Students protested, calling on the government to release or charge him. The government arrested the students and took them to the Red Sea Coast – to a place called Wi'a. The temperature was $45^0$C and two of the students died of sunstroke.

CPE condemned the government for infringing their human rights. It was posted in the Mekelle Tigrinya newspaper. I was singled out for interrogation, accused of conspiring with the G-15 to demonstrate against the government, and instigating the Asmara inhabitants to topple it. I strongly denied the allegation. At last, I was pardoned with a warning not to interfere in government affairs. But after the G-I5 were arrested and no one protested, it was obvious I would be one of the victims of the witch hunt in due course.

At the end of December 2001, CPE was invited to attend a conference in The Hague, Netherlands, and I took it as a lifesaving opportunity. After the conference I made my way to London.

As soon as Berhane heard of my arrival in London, he contacted me and told me that he and other colleagues had started to help the new refugees who escaped repression. I told him I would be glad to join them, but I needed some time to reflect. For me it was a crisis period. My only consolation was that I was alive to continue to struggle for justice and peace. Many of my compatriots became victims during the witch-hunt, were arrested, and to this day, no one knows whether they are alive or dead.

Berhane had recently established the EEPT and he and his colleagues were the first to organise a seminar to expose the human rights violations in Eritrea. He became an inspiration to those who stood up against repression and wanted to support refugees and asylum seekers.'

Amanuel Yemane recalls how Berhane helped to change UK government policy in relation to Eritrean refugees.

## Amanuel Yemane

In 2003, the EEPT held a conference about Eritrean refugees in Sudan. The conference took place in Conway Hall, Red Lion Square, London. Malcolm Harper, former director of the UN Association in the UK, chaired the meeting.

In the previous year, the UN had changed the status of Eritreans, declaring that they would no longer be considered as refugees in Sudan, as Eritrea had achieved independence. The effect was that Sudan would no longer recognise Eritreans who had come to Sudan as refugees, as citizens. So, they were neither citizens nor refugees.

The concern at the time was that other countries might follow the example of Sudan. The aim of the conference was that the refugee status of Eritreans should continue to be recognised, as the conditions of military service were considered by the UN as akin to slavery. Also opponents of the government were subject to arbitrary arrest, indefinite detention and in some cases, disappearance.

A representative of the Home Office attended the conference at Berhane's invitation and Berhane suggested to him that he should visit Eritrea – which he did. In Asmara he interviewed diplomats, NGO representatives and citizens.

Following his visit, the Home Office recognised that anyone who came from Eritrea would be accepted unconditionally as a refugee as long as they hadn't asked for asylum in another European country. This had the effect of reducing the length of processing applications from a matter of years to a matter of weeks. Before this the Home Office didn't have a policy about Eritrean asylum seekers – applications were treated case by case. This is one of the biggest contributions that Berhane made to asylum seekers.

Berhane was fair and brave when it came to his political stance. Once, the Eritrean ambassador to the UK, Tesfamichael Gerahtu, was invited to Chatham House when he was first appointed. Berhane was one of the speakers and he gave first class respect to the ambassador. Tesfamichael assumed he was a government supporter and went to Berhane and thanked him for his speech. Berhane replied, 'OK, I love you because you are the representative of my country. However, I oppose your government.'

Another time, Meles Zenawi[17] came to Chatham House. Some Ethiopians were at the gate demonstrating and shouting, 'You thief'. Berhane raised his hand after Meles had spoken. He said, 'You have explained to us what you are doing for Ethiopia. Will you explain to the people outside who are calling you a thief, as you are their leader?' Meles didn't reply to this question.

---

[17] President of Ethiopia from 1991 to 1995 and Prime Minister of Ethiopia from 1995 until his death in 2012

Later in 2013, at a meeting of Eritrean intellectuals, despite knowing that Berhane opposed the government, and was Aregawi's[18] friend, Meles said 'Oh Berheen', and hugged him.

On another occasion he brought together all the civil society organisations and political parties in a conference in 2014, to discuss their roles. Before that many would have opposed each other, but Berhane managed something that no-one else could have done: achieve good representation across the board. With a budget of less than £5,000, he managed to bring together people from Ethiopia, Sudan, Europe and the U.S.

Berhane also organised a meeting at Caux for five Eritreans who had left the EPLF and the government, including Ambassador Abdullah Adem and former Defence Minister Mesfin Hagos. Berhane hosted the meeting but did not attend their discussions. He ensured that they had five days to discuss their differences and try to reach a solution.

By all accounts, Berhane was absorbed in his work with Eritrean refugees, and in his conciliation between the various factions involved in the struggles in Ethiopia and Eritrea throughout his time in London. In this, he strove to bring people together regardless of religion, as journalist Yaseen Mohmad Abdalla describes in his commemoration, 'Berhane, the Peace Messenger':

**Yaseen Mohmad Abdalla**

I had heard of Berhane decades ago when he was working in Sudan, but I only got to know him for the first time in London, about eight years before his death.

I remember we met in a hotel in west London at a press conference of a newly-formed Eritrean civil society organisation.

---

[18] Aregawi Berhe, founder member of the Tigray Peoples Liberation Front (TPLF); spent 30 years in exile then returned to Ethiopia in 2018; Head of Tigray Democratic Coalition Party (TAND)

We went together from the meeting place, and he suggested that we go to a café to chat. Since then, we have met from time to time, often at Victoria Station, which we considered a middle ground between our two homes.

Berhane used to call me whenever he visited the area in which I live and ask me if we could meet saying, 'My brother…,' and most often I agreed, as seeing and talking to him was enjoyable. In addition to the political discussions on Eritrea, he used to recount his memories, especially of his time in Sudan. I was surprised that, after several decades, he remembered the names of many Sudanese he had worked with or knew.

On one occasion Berhane suggested that he and I should invite an equal number of Eritrean Muslims and Christians to prepare a meeting of representatives of the two faiths in London. Berhane believed that there was a gap between Muslims and Christians and that such a meeting would help bridge the gap and avoid disputes in the Eritrean community in future.

I was convinced of Berhane's noble motive, but I saw political pitfalls in adopting such a proposal. In addition, I believed that the gap between the followers of the two religions has political and cultural roots that cannot be addressed in the way Berhane suggested. Berhane was not convinced of the reasons for my refusal to participate and continued to present the idea to me. I don't know if Berhane discussed the issue with others, but I haven't heard that such a meeting ever took place.

Berhane's final contribution was the sponsorship by EEPT of a meeting of Eritrean opposition group leaders in London in March 2020. The aim of the meeting was to create an umbrella for joint action against the regime under the revived theme of 'Salvation of the People and their State'. Berhane played the largest role in convening the meeting, making all the arrangements and the necessary contacts to hold it and ensure its success.

Berhane was looking forward very much to the meeting taking place. Unfortunately, at the last minute, the meeting had to be cancelled because of the lockdown. Following this setback, Berhane nevertheless continued to convene discussions via zoom, and the opposition leaders broadcast a declaration in June 2020[19] which still holds. But Berhane's health was already deteriorating by then.

Berhane was like a movable human bridge between Christians and Muslims or between Eritrean lowlanders and highlanders in London. He had extensive relations with the people of the Eritrean lowlands, and he was known among them as Berhane Sudanow, the Sudanese magazine in which he worked during the eighties. He used to attend Muslim occasions, or the events of civil or political organisations that have a predominantly Muslim membership. His good spoken Arabic, and knowledge of Eritrean Muslim cultures was due to his work in the Eritrean lowlands and later in Sudan, and because of that was able to communicate with people originating from those areas.

Maybe the best characteristic of Berhane was his kindness and his heartfelt courtesy. He was kind and caring to everyone. Berhane will be missed by all Eritreans in London, they will miss him on their good and their bad days.

During its first few years, the EEPT became well-known amongst Eritreans, and the link with IofC became increasingly fruitful. In this following account, Ali Hindi describes the characteristics that made Berhane different and outstanding.

**Ali Hindi**

I first met Berhane in 2008 in a shop. We recognised each other as Eritrean, and spoke briefly. After that, Berhane mentioned me to General Mercorios, who had heard of me, and we

---

[19] See Appendix 2

managed to get in contact. The three of us started meeting. Berhane invited me to a workshop at IofC on 'The Theory of Teamwork', with Dr Meredith Belbin.

Berhane, the General and I then continued seeing each other regularly, and became known as 'the three generations'. In 2009 we went to an IofC National Fellowship Weekend in Derbyshire. This was the first time I saw Berhane in action. I recognised his special skills and personality in promoting reconciliation. We were a group of Eritreans, one woman and five guys. That weekend a young woman, Fiona Leggat, whom he knew in connection with IofC, passed away. Berhane was very touched and upset, in tears. I realised I was dealing with somebody with a big heart, with empathy, and ready to listen. He was a man with a very open mind, with no barriers in terms of race and religion – he was universalist. His world view was regardless of doctrine.

Eritreans tend to be rigid in terms of doctrine. We are loyal to our religious convictions and ethnic affiliation. Berhane was ready to challenge this. From an Orthodox Christian background, he had respect for Islam and the Prophet Mohammed, and a great respect for Muslims. This made him unique among Eritrean highlanders. They tend to put up barriers, but Berhane did not, and in this he was isolated. As a young man, he was exposed to the Sudanese, with whom he felt no barriers, given his universal personality.

In our meetings, we never made a full stop, only a comma. In him, I found a moral compass.

With regard to what made him special, Berhane was a nationalist, but it was not based on anger, and this set him apart. He was Eritrean, but also had the Tigray side in his family. He lived at peace with this. Other Eritreans would tend to conceal Tigrayan origins. His attitude was 'I identify in the struggle with Eritreans but will work with Ethiopians'. He always stuck with this and the things he said during the Badme war of 1998-2000. As an Eritrean with Tigrayan heritage his non-sectarianism caused him particular problems with those Eritreans and Tigrayans who took entrenched positions. He said that in going to war successively with its neighbours – Yemen, Ethiopia, Sudan – the Eritrean government was trying to create a common identity, one that actually did not pre-exist colonialism.

When approaching the Eritrean cause, Berhane was in favour of positive discrimination for lowlanders, as highlanders had tended to hold the upper hand. The armed struggle of the EPLF (Eritrean People's Liberation Front) was dominated by highlanders. Berhane ensured that Muslim lowlanders were present in any meeting. When the League of Eritrean Lowlanders was established, Berhane participated, and invited them in turn to meetings he organised or was involved in. That was his special quality. Berhane was part of Highland society, but no other highlander showed a stronger commitment to working inclusively with lowlanders. He saw the combined nationalism as the foundation for any involvement in the region. He started from the nationalist loyalty based on identity, then expanded this to the whole region, and from that, the whole Horn of Africa was his home. However Eritrea is a state now and he recognised and accepted that completely.

Berhane moved in a different direction from aggressive nationalists, to working for a peaceful coexistence amongst communities. He didn't like to upset people, and would aim at compromising at every turn, while retaining the integrity of his beliefs.

By 2009, so many young highlanders were fleeing from Eritrea. Berhane loved his people, but at the same time he wished they would change from their adherence to the government. Amongst the highlanders, family plays a big part – it is the first cell of the nation. This is very positive if there is good governance. There is an agricultural mentality, with high standards of moral conduct and moral values, which prohibit corruption, wrongdoing or killing. These standards are undermined by poor government. If an individual identifies themself as being different in their thinking from the norm, as Berhane did, they face isolation, as he did.

The lowlanders do not have conformity to this extent. During Ramadan, they cannot break the fast, but otherwise there is more leniency. So lowlanders do not have that pressure in Muslim culture, that highlanders have in the Orthodox culture. Berhane was a critic of highlanders' aggressive tendencies. He enjoyed lowlanders' compromising skills and abilities. He was more joyful when meeting with lowlanders, and more ebullient. To me, he was a lowland Sudanese, born in the highlands.

Was Berhane a pacifist? I would say not entirely, he had strong values and would do anything to defend them. He would compromise in order to avoid conflict. His degree of pacifism would far outweigh his being pro-war. My lasting impression is that he would go to a big extent to keep the peace, rather than be aggressive. I can see he was drawn to the Quakers, who are pacifist. Also, Sufiism made a strong impact on Berhane, and he was an admirer of Rumi.

What should we be doing to carry on Berhane's legacy? I would say, working more with young Eritreans. Berhane always had his feet on the ground and approached his work with humility. He would act in a way that is necessary to the times. After Meles' death, he brought Eritreans and Ethiopians together to see what relationship there might be between them after that. His last involvement was to bring the Eritrean opposition parties together, at their invitation, with a full mandate. He told me this would be his final project.

Berhane was a bridge between highlanders and lowlanders. We need to send a message to the highlanders to embrace

Berhane's approach towards positive discrimination. We should carry on working with Horn of Africa groups, and not let our Eritrean nationality make us isolated. Working with the young is of the greatest importance.

Ali Hindi stresses the importance of working with the young. Here Amanuel Yemane describes a youth project that EEPT ran in 2003, which shows that it did not just confine itself to the adult sphere.

## Bridging the Gap: EEPT Community Project

In 2003, EEPT ran a very successful project called Bridging the Gap. The project brought Eritrean parents (mostly from south London) and their young children together to discuss their culture, values and heritage.

The Gap (challenge) was that the parents, who were first-generation immigrants, wanted to raise their children in the Eritrean culture and values, whereas the youngsters were not interested and thought them outdated.

However, there was a bigger challenge in creating an atmosphere where there could be an exchange of ideas, as most of the youngsters would not bother to turn up to a meeting or workshop. After exploring different ideas, it was agreed that football was the best way to attract them.

Two teams, one for ages 10-13 and another 14-17 were set up and started regular training with complete kits. As expected, the young people came on board and attended two workshops which helped create an atmosphere where both sides managed to appreciate and respect each other's positions. As part of the programme, parents and their children were given a tour of Old Trafford, the home of Manchester United. The project was the brainchild of Berhane, and it wouldn't have happened without his knowledge and valuable skills, especially communicating with young people.

# Working with Ugandans in London

Berhane also worked with other refugee communities and for several years was involved with the USDI (Uganda Sustainable Development Initiative). This account by Josephine Apira, chair of the organisation, describes the contribution Berhane was able to make.

## Josephine Apira

The story starts with one of many memorable moments of interaction with Berhane which took place just before the Covid-19 lockdown on 12th-14th March 2020. USDI (Uganda Sustainable Development Initiative) organised a three-day training for its members at IofC's London centre, on Leadership and Nation-Building. The training was adapted from the RRB (Refugees as Re-Builders)[20] course to meet the specific needs of the Ugandan community.

Participants arrived with many doubts and questions of what to expect from the training. The day began with a calming introduction from IofC and a thought-provoking film, followed by exciting selected topics. One of them was 'Identifying root causes of divisions and developing strategies for trust-building' facilitated by Berhane.

From his previous study of Eritrean diaspora case studies, Berhane facilitated two powerful sessions on the topic. His sessions went past the allocated time due to the interest generated. Sadly, this was to be the last event with Berhane. At the end of the day, the feedback was that there was good bonding and understanding between trainees and the facilitator. These experiences added to USDI's way of working being adopted and replicated in diaspora and at home.

---

[20] IofC training course

Berhane's interaction with the Ugandan community began much earlier. In the autumn of 2012, outside the hall where the African Economic Summit was taking place in London, Ugandan communities were holding a peaceful protest against the lack of democracy, unjust governance, Human Rights abuses, and arbitrary arrest and detention in Uganda.

Many politicians, diplomats and journalists walked past the protesters, but Berhane went up to the Ugandans and engaged with them. He was interested in finding out what was happening in Uganda and in the community. He took pictures and recordings from members who were happy that at least one journalist was interested in listening to them.

Unlike recent disappointing responses and reporting from journalists on Uganda, Berhane appeared different and genuine, and encouraged further meetings to understand what was going on in the country.

After consultation with the community, it was agreed that leaders could meet with Berhane to further understand how to work with him. As a journalist Berhane had a good knowledge about Uganda, and was very specific when comparing issues of governance, democracy and freedom with the situation in his own country and community. He had an international outlook with regard to African countries, especially the Horn and East African countries.

It took several meetings and a couple of years to build trust with Berhane. But he kept his promises, and kept time, making it possible to progress. He had a genuine interest when communicating with people and creating space and time to meet, listening and understanding the storyline.

Ugandans know that public information about stability and economic success in the country is greatly exaggerated, and the dire situation that ordinary citizens face is concealed. Berhane became convinced that there were issues in the country and made efforts to find opportunities for meetings with his contacts. After three or four years, he encouraged the leaders of our group to join the weekly AfR (Agenda for Reconciliation) meetings at IofC to share concerns with other community groups in similar situations.

Berhane's flexibility and sensitive responses enabled the move to join the AfR meetings from 2014 up to the present. It has been reported that some community members still occasionally meet in South London, having been introduced to each other by Berhane. With Berhane's support and encouragement, USDI was established at the IofC centre and continues with its activities, meetings, trainings, workshops, and conferences.

In the area of unity and leadership, his knowledge and humorous advice was amazing. In one of the meetings when the discussion on unity and leadership was not moving, we called Berhane for advice. He said that as a stand-alone these topics can be tricky but that, from his experience, most countries still have loyalty to ethnic groups or parties. If their leaders can be identified, there may be some among them who would be willing to meet with others and achieve a common understanding. That could be the beginning of finding a leader for the whole community.

One of his key pieces of advice was, 'Do not prescribe' – firstly, let everyone talk and let the known facts come from them. Then you can draw a road map, and they will own it.

He encouraged us to keep the spirit of 'We can do it', which he sees amongst our team. He advised that we should get access to some media or TV journalists who can help to highlight issues about Uganda. He also advised us to get rid of emotions and stick to facts that people want to know about, e.g., land, human rights, education, healthcare services, investments etc. USDI later organised a successful conference based on that guidance and the common understanding which drew a huge response and gave direction for further actions by the organisation.

From his own country and experience of working with war-affected people from different countries, he got to know some USDI members individually who saw him as their mentor, teacher and friend.

There is no doubt about his wisdom and leadership. While away on a trip he still managed to send a text to USDI members saying, 'Congratulations for the successful conference! Keep it up. You are not alone.' Likewise, he was away on a working trip when a documentary film on Uganda was shown at the IofC centre, he texted that since he now knew the Ugandan situation, he felt our pain, and hoped that change would be near.

Berhane had a wealth of knowledge and he seemed to read a lot. We found that he was running a Tigrinya language course at SOAS and worked for many years as an interpreter in courts of law. He was remarkable in being able to speak at least four languages.

USDI has evolved into a worldwide organisation under many names, carrying on the work of education, advocacy and trust-building as a social action for change in Uganda. Change will come to Uganda, and Berhane played a key role in making the change happen and we are grateful for that. The sudden news about his deteriorating health was a shock to many, and his passing was a huge loss.

After hearing the sad news of Berhane's death, members expressed their loss over the phone and commented on the qualities he had and how they saw him. One said, 'Berhane was so close to all of us, a remarkable man, may his soul rest in eternal peace.' Another said, 'Berhane was a legend to many in the diaspora communities. He stood firm to see that USDI becomes a beacon of hope. The gap Berhane left will be a huge challenge to fill. May the Almighty grant him eternal peace.' And another said, 'We share the pain together with the family, may he rest in peace.'

One senior member remembers, 'Berhane was a man with an eagle eye, always able to spot an African woman in distress. That is how he spotted our chair during the activities of exposing human rights violations in our country, and he went on to introduce her to IofC and help to build the organisation. From that day we attached ourselves to IofC and this relationship has cemented our unity on a daily basis, and across the diaspora worldwide and at home.'

I had the honour of knowing Berhane for over six years and later met his family, his sister Haimanot and the nieces. They are so loving and genuine, just like Berhane. I am happy that Haimanot fulfilled Berhane's wishes to see and meet many of his community and friends and cared for him up to the last day.

Our memory of Berhane is that of a kind-hearted, loving, humorous friend to many. We all miss him. MHSRIP.

## Teaching, translating, interpreting and supporting new migrants

As well as his continuous activities with refugee communities in London, Berhane was a university lecturer, teacher, translator and interpreter. He was a sessional lecturer of Tigrinya and Amharic languages at SOAS, an examiner with the Chartered Institute of Linguists, an assessor of interpreting and translation for students' glossaries for the Mary Ward Centre and the Workers Educational Association. He was also a trainer for the Language Services Direct, whose customers include diplomats from the Foreign and Commonwealth Office.

He was also a human rights researcher for Africa Watch/Human Rights Watch on the Horn of Africa, a Programme Officer for IFAA (Institute for African Alternatives), a teacher of Maths and ESOL at Blackfriars Settlement, an asylum case worker for the Migrant Helpline in Ashford, and an interpreter for Amnesty International.

In 2001, Berhane gave an interview to his friend Jane Mace, who was also a colleague in the Language and Literacy Unit. Jane, who, sadly, died in 2022, wrote extensively about language and included this passage from Berhane in her book 'The give and take of writing – scribes, literacy and everyday life'[21].

## Jane Mace

Berhane, a friend who had worked as a translator and transcriber for Amnesty International, told me:

There were things like reports from prison. It's – sometimes – you get tortured when you read. You get letters from prison, graphically describing how they were tortured. The last one I was given – about 82 pages – I had to give to some friends, because after a while I could not take it. These friends are also very good translators. And then I would check it myself.

'Do you think it was less painful for them?' I asked.

No, but at least we shared the pain.

Berhane also spoke of the additional work of the translator – the one who must find the means to transpose a text between two languages. Not only was he transcribing the words (originally spoken in Amharic or Tigrinya), he was also having to translate them into English. The choices are subtle; the

---

[21] The give and take of writing-scribes, literacy and everyday life, Jane Mace, 2002, NIACE, Leicester

scribe can shift out of an emotional engagement with the text into an intellectual struggle with language:

> In the process of selecting a word, you get involved. It's like building in our country. Of course here, every brick comes from a factory and therefore they are all the same. But buildings in Eritrea or Ethiopia, because all the stones are different shapes, you have to adjust the position of the stone... So what do they do? They try to adjust it. If the first stone, or the surrounding stones, are given a certain shape, they will come with a stone that will fill that... So when one translates, you have various synonyms and when you have to select the one that will fit, you get involved... Like, the other day I was thinking about: 'agreement', 'convention', 'pact', 'accord'. Each one has a different shade of meaning.

Berhane worked for some time with the Migrant Helpline in Dover, advising asylum seekers about legal, medical and housing support. He provided cultural orientation, for example, informing new arrivals that the British used 'please' and 'thank you' in speech more often than Eritreans, so he advised using both frequently, to avoid the perception that they were rude.

## Family

During his time in London, Berhane travelled several times to Ethiopia. In Addis in 1994 he was re-united with his sister Tsegai, and nearly twenty years later he met his two sisters Askale and Tsblets and their families in Tigray. He was unable to go to Eritrea and visit his mother, apart from a few days in 1994. However, she travelled to London to stay in Kennington with Berhane and Amanda for three months in 2002.

Berhane's eldest son Yemane had settled in the US with his mother, and lives there now with his wife and children. Berhane's second son Medhanie, and daughter Fewien, grew up in Germany with their mother. His third son Hadish grew up in Sheffield with his mother.

During the 2000s, Berhane's family members based in the UK increased. His youngest son Jonathan and his mother Fana settled in Scotland.

Berhane's sister Haimanot and her family also came. The first of them to arrive, in 2000, was her eldest daughter Abeba. Haimanot followed later, as did her three other children, Semhar, Selam and Amanuel, and her eldest grandchild. Haimanot's family, including three more grandchildren, now all live in London. This provided Berhane with the companionship of close family for the last ten years of his life.

## A sisterly view

Berhane's sister, Haimanot, followed Berhane to London in July 2009. She remembers:

> Berhane was well connected and helped me with finding solicitors and with other support. He was very busy and even though we were living in the same city we didn't see each other as much as we would have liked. Community work about peace and reconciliation for the whole Horn of Africa particularly among Eritreans was very important to him and took a lot of his time – sometimes at the expense of his family.

> We used to spend Christmas and Easter at my house together and he used to say, 'I will come next week and we can talk all night,' but he then ended up talking to his friends in America or Europe on the phone all night. Then I would say, 'What is the point of coming here to spend time with me, but end up talking to your friends instead?' As usual with Berhane, he would smile and say, 'What can I do? He called me and one thing led to another.' It was the same even if we met in a restaurant or café – he would end up talking on the phone to someone. However, I always cherished the five or ten minutes we spent together talking and laughing. He never called me Haimanot. He always called me 'Haimanot haftey' (my sister).

# West Yorkshire

Berhane's London base gave him the chance to exercise his gifts and brought some personal contentment. However, his happy place in the UK was the area he called 'West Yorkshire': this referred specifically to Hebden Bridge, Todmorden and Walsden where he enjoyed staying on many occasions and found peace and relaxation. The landscape, with its rugged hills and cairns, stone-built houses and rocky waterfalls reminded him of the Eritrea of his childhood. Buildings in West Yorkshire were usually made from stone, not bricks. He noted with regret that his native country had suffered immensely from deforestation since his childhood, while the post-industrial north was being re-forested.

Berhane expressed the wish to be buried in West Yorkshire. In the event, this was not to be, and he is buried in Mortlake Cemetery in London. Amanda Woolley and Christine Brown designed and placed a memorial to Berhane in Wainsgate Cemetery in Old Town, Hebden Bridge, a place he visited shortly before his death.

## Faith matters

Berhane was raised in the Orthodox faith, but said his faith was loosened by his encounter with Marxist politics during the independence struggles of his youth. However, he was always drawn to spirituality and religion. He worked briefly in London with a group called FAR (Faith Asylum Refugee Network) and appreciated the ecumenical spirit of co-operation that they advocated. He encountered Quakers as development workers in Sudan and later attended some Quaker meetings in Sheffield. In London, he trained in the mid-'90s as a mediator for Lambeth Council, on a course run by the Streatham Quakers. He went regularly to Westminster Quaker Meetings for a few years. Michael Bartlet recalls his long association with this Meeting, including Berhane's participation for years in monthly country walks, led by the late Keith Gibson.

## Michael Bartlet

I had the pleasure of knowing Berhane as a member of Westminster Quaker Meeting for about fifteen years. More recently we shared the experience of both being teachers at SOAS. Berhane was for many years a valued participant in Saturday Quaker walks where a community of friends enjoyed rambling conversations across the English Countryside, often sharing a pub or picnic lunch, returning in the evening to London.

Berhane's first-hand experience of political turmoil in Eritrea gave him an authority and urbanity on these suburban rambles whether mocking the myopia of the 'war on terror' or exploring the dilemmas of pacifism. His rich hinterland and varied life made him a fascinating companion who never lost a radical commitment to the cause of refugees and exiles.

Berhane's authentic spirituality in more occasional spoken ministry was an inspiration to many who attended Westminster Meeting at 52 St Martin's Lane. I remember a mutual friend sharing the impression left by Berhane's meditation on how the surface beauty of Monet's Water Lily cycle would be impossible without the innumerable invisible tendrils reaching into the darkness and depths of the fecund mud beneath.

Eventually Berhane returned to the faith of his youth. He visited India for an IofC conference in 2014. There he met a Sufi mystic and credited her with bringing him back to his Orthodox practice. From then on, he prayed alone in his room, rather than attending church, and always wore a wooden orthodox cross round his neck.

Throughout Berhane's time in London, he connected with Andy Gregg through his father, Dr Ian Gregg. Andy's tribute, and that of Yohannes Asmelash, complete this chapter.

## Andy Gregg

Berhane expressed his views without rancour or discord and was always dignified and considerate. Throughout his life he had many friendships with a wide variety of Eritreans and Sudanese and other African and diaspora groups as well as Europeans. He maintained friends in both the Eritrean liberation fronts, EPLF and ELF, at a time when they viewed each other with mutual suspicion and often outright and dangerous hostility.

He had a strong commitment to peace-making and conflict resolution and for the last decades of his life was involved in IofC. In 2011, I attended a residential conference at Caux along with Berhane and several other human rights and peace activists from Eritrea and elsewhere. Berhane's contribution was hugely welcomed and his sensitive and open treatment of people with a variety of views and perspectives was very much in evidence. Berhane was a very sociable person and always had a sparkle in his eye and interesting things to say. We enjoyed many social events as well as walks in Hertfordshire together with other friends from the refugee sector and from diverse backgrounds.

He is hugely missed, and I am glad that his unique experiences are being captured by his friends and colleagues.

## Yohannes Asmelash

I have lost many good friends over the years and Berhane is one of them. I have known him since 1994 and we were very close friends till he passed away.

Berhane always said that he learned to be a teacher and he had no other ambition other than to be a teacher. He was indeed a very good teacher. He was a very good reader and as a result he accumulated a wealth of knowledge in various academic areas. If I asked Berhane about anything, he would either give me an answer or he would refer me to someone who could. He was my reference.

Berhane took several initiatives in regard to reconciling and bringing together all or at least most of the Eritrean political organisations in opposition. Although he was not affiliated to any of them, he always thought that a united front under one umbrella organisation was for the good of the people who are looking for change.

His participation in the first congress of the Eritrean National Council for Democratic Change Congress in November 2011 in Awasa, Ethiopia, was driven by that belief. He still thought a lot needed to be done to consolidate the results of the congress and thus he was prepared to do more. Hence, his participation and also his moderation of a panel discussion of all the representatives of the political organisations at the conference in Frankfurt in April 2019. This was one of his historic contributions to bringing together all the Eritrean political organisations.

To solidify the good will of all Eritrean political organisations at the Frankfurt conference, he thought of the even bigger plan of organising a conference for all the political organisations to take place in London. Unfortunately, whilst the preparation was underway and a venue booked for March 2020, Covid-19 struck. I was working with him preparing the invitation letters. Sadly, the London Conference to be convened in person did not happen. Instead, it took place via Zoom (still called the London Conference) in June 2020, and a new entity was formed in July 2020 called the Eritrean Political Forces Coordinating Committee. Berhane will be greatly missed by all peace and justice seekers.

May his soul rest in peace.

# Berhane's last days

Until mid-March 2020, Berhane was preparing for the London conference, which could not take place due to COVID. He spent the first three months of lockdown with Amanda in West Yorkshire, walking every day for miles in the beautiful surrounding countryside. As related earlier, he was able to conduct discussions during this time with Eritrean opposition groups on Zoom, leading to the London Declaration of June 2020. He was also in contact with his grandchildren in the USA.

After he received his terminal diagnosis in June, Amanda brought him to London to spend his last days in Haimanot's home where he had the support of family and friends. It was a fine summer and while he was able, he could meet people outside, enjoying Haimanot's garden and many local walks. Berhane died in Haimanot's house on 26 October 2020.

*Chapter editor: Amanda Woolley.*

Berhane at home, London, mid-
1990s (AW)

Berhane in London, 1990s (AW)

Berhane and Nyeya Yen, London
(AY)

Ali Hindi, at Initiatives of
Change (AY)

Berhane at a meeting in London (AW)

General Mecorios, Russom, Petros Tesfagiorgis, and Berhane,
GHARWEG 2000s. (AY)

Amanuel Yemane and Berhane, Bridging the Gap trip to
Old Trafford (AY)

Berhane near Arundel, West
Sussex (AW)

Cover of 'Mizan', Tigrinya
language magazine (AY)

Berhane in the countryside with friend, Ingrid (taken by AW)

Berhane and his sister
Haimanot, London

Berhane and his mother
Tebereh, Oakden Street,
London 2002 (AW)

Berhane on 'Refugees are Welcome' demonstration, London, 2016
(AW)

Berhane, Quaker Centre, Euston, London, 2018 (AW)

Berhane on a Westminster Quaker walk: Seven Sisters, late 1990s: Amanda Woolley, Shahida Khan, Berhane, Aregawi Berhe (AW)

Berhane outside an Orthodox church, Tigray (AY)

Berhane at Axum, Tigray (AY)

Berhane and Amanda at Stoodley Pike (peace memorial), West
Yorkshire, mid-1990s (AW)

Berhane playing football, Old Town, West Yorkshire (AW)

Berhane near Hebden Bridge, West Yorkshire (AW)

Berhane, Christine and Laurie Brown, Old Town, June 2020 (AW)

Berhane and Yohannes Asmelash at the Elephant and Castle

Berhane as moderator of the conference of Eritean political
organisations in Frankfurt in April 2019, with fellow delegates

Berhane speaking at the Frankfurt conference, April 2019

Berhane and Haimanot in London, July 2020(AW)

Berhane and Abeba in Haimanot's garden, July 2020 (AW)

Berhane, taken by Amanda, at Riverside Studios, July 2020 (AW)

Chapter Five

# Berhane, Eritrean Peacemaker

## Building bridges and bringing his people together

In the last 20 years of his life, Berhane found a calling, tools and a base from which to help reconcile the people of the Eritrean diaspora in preparation for the time when it might be possible for them to return and help rebuild their homeland.

The seeds were sown in 1978 when he had a chance encounter in Khartoum with an Englishman, Jim Baynard-Smith.

Jim's initial contact with Sudan had been during two years of National Service in the late 1940s as ADC[22] to the Governor General of Sudan. He then studied at Oxford University where he became committed to MRA (Moral Re-Armament)[23], its standards of honesty, purity, unselfishness and love, and the morning practice of seeking Divine guidance.

Drawing on his experience in Sudan, he began to make friends with Africans at the university and he realised that previously he had held a superior attitude towards Africans. Repairing relationships between the British and the peoples of the continent became his calling. He later spent several years in Eritrea with his wife Sally – 'By invitation rather than occupation' as he used to say. It was on one of his pastoral visits to Sudan that Jim met

---

[22] Aide-de-Campe – secretary or personal assistant to senior military, government or police officer
[23] Now known as IofC (Initiatives of Change)

85

Berhane – and through another chance meeting, they reconnected in London in the early 1990s.

At Jim's invitation, Berhane occasionally attended gatherings at MRA's centre in Victoria, London. There he began to discover a network of people committed to living by the 'standards' and 'quiet times' and seeking to build trust across the world's divides.

In the summer of 2000, Jim took him to a conference entitled AfR (Agenda for Reconciliation) at MRA's international centre in Caux, near Geneva, Switzerland – a place where French and Germans first began to reconcile after the Second World War.

Jim was a member of the preparation team for those annual conferences which were based at the MRA centre in London, and Berhane began to attend its weekly meetings.

**The following extracts from the minutes of subsequent AfR meetings show the development of Berhane's calling as a peacemaker, and how he goes about building a network.**

A minute in January 2001 records Berhane as informing the team 'that a group of Eritreans have formed an Eritrean Reconciliation Forum. They have appealed to AfR for facilitation in a quiet place where a group of Eritreans could move beyond mere politics towards a common understanding.'

In February 2002[24], on Jim's invitation, he attended a preparation meeting for that summer's AfR conference in Caux, and volunteered to be a member of the planning group for a plenary meeting on 'Answering Anger, Fear and Mistrust'.

At a subsequent weekly AfR meeting in London, Jim reported that Berhane 'would like to take 10-12 [Eritreans] to Tirley Garth[25] on

---

[24] By this time MRA had been re-named Initiatives of Change (IofC)
[25] IofC's conference centre in Cheshire

27-29th April, facilitated by AfR, and hopes to take three or four to Caux at a time when relations are difficult between Ethiopia and Eritrea and within Eritrea.'

After the conference in Caux, an AfR meeting minute in September records that Berhane 'wants to continue work started with Brig. Gen. Mercorios Haile[26], retired Eritrean deputy commander of the Ethiopian Air Force'.

In June 2003, Berhane appears on the programme of a two-day internal AfR gathering including Gen. Joseph Lagu[27] in a briefing entitled 'Focus on the Greater Horn'. The minute reports Berhane as saying that 'Thanks to Jim (Baynard-Smith), there have been meetings initially to bring Ethiopians and Eritreans together – [but that] proved almost impossible because of the need to clean own back yard, and bring Eritrean groups together. The core group is still there, but we did not advance as much as we expected.' After this General Mercorios Haile also begins to attend the weekly AfR meetings.

On 21st May 2005 Berhane organised a one-day conference on the theme, 'Eritrea and Ethiopia: A way forward' at the Al Kuffa Conference Hall in Bayswater. At that time there was a real fear that Ethiopia and Eritrea might go to war again over the disputed border area of Badme.

Describing his aim for the event, Berhane said he would like to see the conference 'produce a level of continuity similar to that of the Somali group'. He was referring to a parallel development in the Somali community, in which Hon. Osman Jama Ali, former deputy prime minister of Somalia had gathered a group of Somali

---

[26] Gen. Mercorios Haile, Eritrean former Deputy Commander of the Ethiopian Airforce who founded around 40 community centres in the UK for Eritrean communities

[27] Former leader of the south Sudanese rebellion and later Vice-President of Sudan

clan leaders which had just concluded a series of weekend meetings leading to the founding of Somali Initiative for Dialogue and Democracy.[28]

The conference was chaired by Dr Mohamed Suliman, Sudanese Director of the IFAA (Institute for African Alternatives). Sir Jim Lester MP[29] opened the conference, and the keynote address by Lorne Braun[30] was on 'Eritrea and Ethiopia: Identities and Dialogues'. It was followed by discussion and questions with two panels, one with Ato Aregawi Berhe, Dr Tesfa Mehari, Ato Ghiday Zeratsion, followed by another with General Mercorios Haile, Ato Woldeamanuel Hankerso[31] and Sir Jim Lester. Dr Richard Greenfield, Professor of History at Oxford University spoke about his recent visit to Asmara.

Reflecting on the conference, Berhane expressed his disappointment with how few Ethiopians had attended. The AfR minute records him as saying, 'There were others who, if they had come, would have protested violently. But only one protested, and he later phoned to apologise. For many it was too soon to start [talking] as the border issue is still unresolved. If the propaganda for war is like a balloon, this meeting can be like a small pin. Those who thought there is no other way can now see an alternative. There was an encouraging absence of recrimination and an acceptance of personal and group responsibility for the way forward. As one participant said, 'We must start with ourselves.' Apparently, after the meeting, a group had continued in informal discussion on the failure of the recent talks on the border dispute,

---

[28] Ten Years of Somali Peacemaking in Diaspora – the Story of Somali Initiatives of Dialogue and Democracy (available on the For A New World website)

[29] Veteran Conservative politician who served for 15 years on the Parliamentary Foreign Affairs committee

[30] Canadian expert in international development

[31] Founder of the Ethiopian Sidamo Liberation Movement

and the serious threat by the UN to withdraw its military peace-keeping presence by the end of this month for another four hours.

Berhane is noted as saying: 'The time has come to continue and develop our people-to-people meetings in London, to build trust and communication. But unless each of the participants becomes a 'free' person we may not be effective. Better to have a few of us who trust each other than many who just talk!'

Woldeamanuel Hankerso responded: 'I would underline this strongly, having over a period of time reached a position of confidence and friendship with Berhane, where there was much initial suspicion. Now we two, with General Mercorios Haile, are able to work together because we understand and respect each other's spirit and motives. It is the urgent moment for some of us in the diaspora to engage in open-hearted dialogue individually in this way.'

That summer of 2005, Berhane took three Eritreans, Girmai Mebrahtu, Tzeggai Deres, Abeba Tesfagiorgis, and an Ethiopian, Woldeselassie Asfaw to the AfR conference in Caux.

The next mention of Berhane's attendance at an AfR meeting was on 6 February 2007 when preparations were being made for the visit in May of senior Algerian diplomat Mohamed Sahnoun. Berhane mentioned that he has invited a small group of Eritrean colleagues to a private dinner with Ambassador Sahnoun.

The dinner took place on 3$^{rd}$ May and, apart from Berhane, those present were Berehe Fessehaye (former director in Eritrean Ministry of Finance), Mesfin Ma'alo (Ethiopian Coffee Board in UK) Gebru Tesfamariam (former employee of Eritrean government), Girmai Mebrahtu (former Head of Logistics of UK Branch of Eritrean Relief Association of EPLF), Berhane Gebrenegus (businessman in Eritrea and Ethiopia), Habtegiorgis Abraha (community leader in UK, former senior member of ELF), Abrahaley Mebrahtu (chief accountant to IofC-UK),

Suleiman Hussein (Chairman of Eritrean human rights organisation in UK), Amanuel Eyasu (founder of Assenna Radio), Idris O. Dawd (chief accountant for a charity in London), Dr Yohannes Lijam (physician at Welcome Foundation, UK).

The minutes of the meeting concluded that: 'There was a feeling among Eritreans that Ambassador Sahnoun was speaking frankly as in a discussion between brothers. He appreciated the initiative and the Eritreans were grateful for his kindness and understanding. We left happy realising that we found a knowledgeable and powerful potential supporter.'

A further mention of Berhane in the AfR minutes was on 26 June when he and Woldeamanuel Hankerso 'left early to attend a vigil organised by the Orthodox Church at St Mary's Church, Paddington in support of the Eritrean Patriarch who is under house arrest.[32]'

At an AfR meeting on 27 March 2008, Berhane expressed the close bond that he had with the Somalis he met during the AfR meetings: 'I am inspired by my Somali brothers. We have more or less the same problems at community level and can rely on support from them.' He announced a one-day seminar on team-building on 5th April. It is an attempt to bring groups including community leaders to think together about our community in a more systematic way.' General Mercorios added: 'We are gathering people from different movements, Christian and Muslim, from ELF, EPLF, different regions, people of good will – we have never seen such a good response!'

The following week, Berhane expanded on his vision: 'We as leaders of the Eritrean community have failed our people – we didn't do as much as we should as early as we should. We hope that those who are rising community leaders will pick this up. Despite the increasing number of Eritrean asylum seekers to UK,

---

[32] Abune Antonios 1927-2022

there are fewer in colleges or universities in the UK. We have a high number of offenders, and the government has said that any offender who receives less than a one-year sentence can serve in the community providing there is a viable community. But the Eritreans are not a viable community! We hope to raise our community to that level and take responsibility for our citizens. This would be a blessing!'

## What were Berhane's calling and qualities?

During his last two decades, Berhane's calling gradually clarified into the aim of reconciling the opposition leaders as a means of reconciling the Eritrean people in country and in diaspora. He pursued this using the tools and assets offered by IofC.

In his last years, he had won the confidence of the principal opposition leaders and was able to host online meetings among them. He felt so confident of the trust that had been built between the five leaders, that he decided that he should withdraw from the meetings and let them hammer out the final declaration. Berhane felt that he was on the verge of achieving his life's ambition. But for the UK government's announcement of lockdown due to the COVID-19 pandemic, all five leaders would have journeyed to IofC's London centre where they would made a common declaration on 29th March 2020. Nevertheless, Berhane's legacy endured, and he and the leaders continued their talks on zoom, finally making the declaration three months later[33].

Regarding the qualities that Berhane brought to his later life – nature and nurture – the chapter on Berhane's childhood, combining his own memories with Dr Solomon's and Haimanot's, gives a delightful picture of a cheerful, gregarious, energetic, intelligent, enquiring, generous, helpful little boy. His mother's acceptance of him playing with the Muslims in the police

---

[33] See Appendix 2

compound where he lived, must have contributed to his later openness to people of all religions and cultures.

But there are bleaker tones of a blood feud, shortage of money and food, and instability around him, developing his resilience. His independence emerges when he refuses to accept his father's wish for him to be a lawyer rather than be a teacher.

During his time in Ethiopia, his political engagement increases, and he shows courage in taking part in demonstrations against the regime of Emperor Haile Selassie. His opposition to the Dergue finally causes him to become a refugee in Sudan. Journalism enters his life, developing his understanding of the wider Horn of Africa, and his compassion for people who were passing through extreme hardship. Navigating the dynamics of the Sudanese political class must have sharpened his capacity to read people. And becoming a refugee for the second time, this time in Britain, must have again tested his resilience.

From his time in Sudan, Berhane was drawn to Quakerism, with its emphasis on quiet, gathered worship and self-reflection, pacifism and acceptance of people regardless of who they are.

Similarly, there must have been something in IofC that attracted and held him for two decades. Jim Baynard-Smith's enduring mentorship of him must have been part of it. The supportive AfR network of people from the Horn of Africa, refugees like him, must have played a part. The ethos of the standards and quiet times building trusting relationships, must have been part of it.

There was also a tested approach to nation-building, going back to IofC's experience after the Second World War. These were based on bottom-up and top-down processes of identifying and sustaining relationships with potential partners of integrity and including them in wider networks to enhance their individual contributions.

There were more tangible assets that IofC could offer: a base at the IofC centre in central London where he could gather people for small or large meetings; the conference centres in Cheshire, Switzerland and India; training programmes in Dialogue Facilitation, Team-building and the Refugees as Re-Builders course; also the connections with parliamentarians, diplomats and journalists, not just in the UK but other countries.

Berhane incorporated all these resources and more into his own unique style. His laid-back attitude and his humour would defuse tension in the room and draw everyone together. Everyone looked forward to seeing him arrive at an AfR meeting, and wait to hear him say something that would shock them by its outrageousness, knowing deep down that it would turn out not to be true – like calling his close Ethiopian friend, Ato Betana Hamano, his 'enemy'!

He was very generous – several times I discovered that he had given away more than perhaps he should have because he felt someone needed it more than he did…

His relaxed demeanour disguised a very sharp and observant mind. He maintained friendly relations with leading figures in the community while not becoming identified with any one party. This led them to trust that they wouldn't be put in a difficult situation. And he was skilled in choosing just the right topic that would interest them, but not so sensitive as to cause discomfort. The constant background to all this work was his frequent contact with the main players, encouraging them and sensing what was in their minds.

Berhane has helped me understand what Jesus might have meant by 'Blessed are the Peacemakers'. Berhane brought people together. He kept hope alive, that enemies could become friends.

It was a pleasure and an honour to work with him.

*Peter Riddell, Convenor, Agenda for Reconciliation, IofC UK*

Berhane and Peter Riddell, Barnes, London, July 2020, taken by Haimanot (PR)

Berhane at Caux, Switzerland (IofC conference centre) (AY)

Jim Baynard-Smith and Berhane

Berhane (backrow 2nd from left) with Somali alumni of an IofC
Dialogue Facilitation course (2013) (PR)

Berhane (left) with Somalis on an IofC Dialogue Facilitation course
weekend-away (2014) (PR)

Jim Baynard-Smith (2007) (PR)

Berhane zooming during lockdown, Todmorden, West Yorkshire, May 2020 (AW)

# *Remembering Berhane...*

## Jim Baynard-Smith

I learnt much from Berhane, since we first met in 1978 in Khartoum after his crossing into Sudan, when he helped me understand his wide experience, wisdom and great concern for his beloved Eritrea.

Our friends and colleagues in Initiatives of Change will so much miss his courageous commitment, spirit and humour, and try to share his vision. He is a shining star to guide and encourage us all.

## Mohamed Sharif Mohamud

I am saddened and horrified to know that my dear friend Berhane Woldegabriel has passed away.

By his absence I have lost one of the closest friends I admire. He was amiable, intelligent, full of sense of humour and wholeheartedly attached to the causes that matter to the peoples of Horn Africa and in particular to his home country Eritrea which he loved so much and fought perseveringly to deliver it from its intricate crisis.

He was a formidable leader of his co-citizens and inspired them to fight for a hope and a better future for his country. He was also keenly interested in Somalia, as well as in Ethiopia and was yearning for the three countries to achieve harmonious relations, peace, progress and economic integration.

No one can replace the void he left among us, the Community of the Horn of Africa. May the God Almighty award him his mercy and put his soul to rest.[34]

## David and Elizabeth Locke

Our memories of Berhane are of a very friendly man who was concerned for the plight of his fellow Eritreans. We first met him at Caux, where we were in the same community. He and Amanda came to our home in Tooting. After then we sometimes found ourselves at Caux together.

We often met him at Greencoat Place and he frequently brought us news of Alumseged, who as a refugee had worked with us packing books at the Grosvenor Books offices in Wandsworth. Alum later had an important role in the Police Force of Ethiopia. Berhane always came to the fellowship weekends and encouraged others from the Horn of Africa to be there. We shall miss his cheery greeting. Our lives were enriched by knowing him.

Berhane Woldegabriel R.I.P.

## Goitom Mebrahtu

I knew Berhane in the early '90s. He included me as a committee member when he founded the charity, the Eritrean Education and Publication Trust which helped people from the Horn of Africa to develop their work, life skills and promote conciliation techniques.

He was also part of the Initiatives of Change group and helped us to use their facilities.

---

[34] Mohamed Sharif Mohamud is former Vice-chairman, Somali Initiative for Dialogue and Democracy, and former ambassador of Somalia and Arab League

Berhane introduced me to a great teacher Dr Mohamed Suliman ex-Sudanese Communist Party chairperson who led, along with brother, the Institute for African Alternatives.

In addition to his contributions to our community via his various jobs and roles, Berhane was a modest, very kind and honest man.

## Stephen Yeo

I never worked with Berhane professionally, but often met him with family or friends. He had a unique, unforgettable presence. With an understanding smile in his eyes, he conveyed how pleased he was with every fresh encounter. He always had time to give rather than hurrying on to the next thing. He had original perspectives to offer and much spontaneous wisdom to share. He knew about bits of human experience and activity hundreds of miles from my own, at the same time as being unusually open and curious about things he hadn't (yet) lived or seen. How lucky individuals and whole cultures were to access Berhane's deep skills and empathy as a well-practised resolver of human conflict. Thank you Berhane.

## Lajeel Abdirahman

It has been a while since we heard from each other and believe me, I have no words to express how shocked I was to hear about the death of our dear friend Berhane. I still have his smiling face in front of me. My heart saddens at the very thought that he is no longer with us. I really wanted to join you in the AfR meeting to remember our dear friend. Please pass on my deepest condolences to his family and to all AfR participants.

# Editors' Postscript

Berhane was a proud Eritrean who would have wished to return home if there had been a possibility of a democratic regime. He also felt nostalgic for the Sudan he had known. None of this diminished his affection for London and the UK and his appreciation of the networks and opportunities it afforded him to pursue his goals and enjoy a rich and varied political and social life. He achieved British citizenship in 2001 and was grateful to hold it alongside that of Eritrea. He had the capacity to embrace multiple identities: he felt, at the same time, Eritrean, Habesha and British.

Berhane's work for the last twenty years of his life can be understood in the light of his beliefs that internecine wars and the nationalism they engendered (as opposed to the nationalism of a country fighting to achieve independence from an oppressor) were a disaster for his people and the region.

It was his long-held belief that Christians and Muslims should work together and avoid the traps of inter-faith hostility and fundamentalism. Since his childhood, he had always had Muslim friends and this pattern continued all his life and is attested to in this book. Incidentally he referred to the Bet Israel, the ancient community of Jews in northern Ethiopia, airlifted out of the region by Mengistu in the 1980s and taken to Israel, as 'our cousins'.

Above all, he was a universalist and a humanitarian. He deplored the efforts to blame and stigmatise refugee communities whose plight was the consequence of war and displacement. He worked unceasingly to assist them, imparting his belief that cooperation was empowering and to achieve that you had to accommodate differences and, to use a more recent phrase, disagree agreeably.

# Appendix 1

*Berhane's journalism:*
*articles from Sudanow and Africa World Review*

SUDANOW, July 1977

# The Refugee Problem

*On June 20 Sudan, along with other African countries, commemorated the third African Refugees Day, instituted by the OAU as a yearly event.*

*Sudan plays a special and vital role in the problem of refugees. At present the country is host to about 200,000 Eritrean and 50,000 Ethiopian Refugees, as well as a group of 6,000 who came twelve years ago from what is now Zaire.*

*Refugees from Eritrea and Ethiopia have been entering the country intermittently since 1967, when they fled from the late Emperor Haile*

105

*Selassie's regime. But since the advent of his successors, the military junta of Colonel Mengistu, oppression has increased to such a degree that refugees have flocked across the border.*

*Reporter Berhane Woldegabriel, himself from Eritrea, examines the problems refugees face and looks at the aid organisations operating in Sudan.*

What do the refugees hope for when they enter this country? Where do they go, and what happens to them?

Broadly, they can be divided into three categories: those who are settled in long-stay camps or agricultural development schemes; those who make their way to the towns to find work or continue their studies; and those who intend to leave Sudan for other countries.

All the Eritreans or Ethiopians who enter the country, whether through Port Sudan, Gallabat or Hamdait, are registered at the nearest police station. They are then sorted out: Eritreans to the temporary settlement at Wad el Hillayu, from Gedarens to Um Gulja, eight kms from Gedaref.

Most of them, particularly those with a rural background, remain in these temporary settlement areas where security, food, medicine and education are provided. The policy is that later they are transferred to villages near development schemes where they can work, or they are given enough initial support to attain self-reliance.

The 18,000 Eritreans, mostly nomads, who fled to this country in 1967, were initially aided by $211,900 worth of food commodities by the World Food Programme. They are now living in Gal en Nahal successfully growing simsim and dura.

The group of 6,000 refugees from Zaire who arrived about twelve years ago were settled at Rajaf near Juba with $600,000 of aid from the UNHCR. They are also now economically self-sufficient, and in fact have been so successful that, according to one official, they enjoy a higher standard of living than many of their Sudanese neighbours.

At the moment, a scheme is underway to transfer about 24,000 of the 30,000 refugees who have been living since 1975 at the temporary camp of Wad el Hillayu, only a few kilometres from the

Eritrean border. This is being organised by the Ministry of Interior's Refugee Commissioner's Office, in collaboration with the relief organisations.

Although there are about 2,000 Sudanese farmers near Wad el Hillayu, there is no work there for the refugees. Thus the authorities are resettling them near to developing scheme areas such as Khashm el Girba, Es Suki, and possibly Rahad, where they can readily sell their labour and be self-reliant.

Others will be installed in the Presidential Decree Area where each family will get 10 feddans. UNHCR has also allocated $2.8m for basic infrastructure such as building materials (£s30 per family hut), roads, wells, farm tools, tractors and so on.

The need for self-sufficiency is obvious. Even with the help of relief organisations, a developing country like Sudan cannot support a large number of refugees indefinitely. Relief for refugees is considered to be emergency aid that does not exceed a year. The Eritreans at Wad El Hillayu have already stayed two years and relief can no longer be justified. The World Food Programme has coined a new term, 'quasi-emergency'; it will continue to supply food during the resettlement period and diminish its assistance as the settlers begin to become self-reliant.

The World Food Programme Senior Adviser in Khartoum, Mr Jean-Pierre Noblet said, 'We don't want to produce professional refugees.' 'They have to be transferred,' said Mr Ismail Ibrahim, the Commissioner's Office Representative in Gedaref. 'The food just won't be there after September. Even ERA and ERCCS officials, although they would prefer to see displaced Eritreans living in the liberated areas of their own country, nevertheless agree that the refugees must be self-supporting until they return to Eritrea.

However, most of the refugees at Wad el Hillayu are against the idea of leaving this temporary settlement. The committee of the refugees made this clear during a recent visit to the area by the Ministry of Interior's Commissioner for refugees, Mr Omer Mohamed Ismail and Mr Kozlowski, UNHCR representative in Khartoum. The refugees argue that the Eritrean problem, whose armed struggle against Ethiopia has been going on for 16 years now, will soon be solved and they will be able to go back home. Wad el Hillayu is only a few kilometres from the border; the deeper they move into Sudan they feel their identity will proportionally fade. They also claim that the proposed settlement areas have no adequate water supply and are infested with malaria.

But according to Mr Ismail, the areas have been well studied and Sudanese citizens live in these areas. In fact, a Swedish medical team that went to study the area reported that 'it is even healthier than Wad el Hillayu itself,' he said with a somewhat cynical smile. Some refugees who want to be moved suggest that the refugee team leaders who are responsible for the weekly distribution of rations, are most strongly against the *new* idea, and to maintain their own interests they disseminate such stories. But the team leaders, like the rest, know that the World Food Programme and the UNHCR cannot go on supplying relief to people who could be self-supporting.

Some refugees can only see a political solution. 'We wouldn't have any of this trouble if only the world would rally behind the Eritrean cause and get rid of Mengistu's regime,' said Wadi May Guaila, a refugee at Wad el Hillayu.

Meanwhile, there are the problems encountered by relief operations everywhere. Medical facilities are good, with more than five clinics operating in Wad el Hillayu, but food supply is often irregular.

Delay of supplies is common. Recently, nothing but medical supplies arrived for over a month. As this coincided with the resettlement drive, many refugees saw it as a deliberate attempt to pressurize them.

It was in fact just an unfortunate coincidence. Mr Noblet explained that there are not enough silos, either at Port Sudan or at the camps. Thus consignments have to be carefully-timed, which is not always possible. And there is the problem of conveyance from the port. 'There are certainly food commodities still waiting for transportation from Port Sudan,' said Mr Michel Barton, UNHCR representative at Gedaref.

In 85 cases out of 100, according to a settlement officer in Gedaref, refugees with an urban background leave the settlement areas very soon for the major cities such as Khartoum and Port Sudan. There, they either look for work or a place to study, or they try to go abroad. It is not an easy matter for a refugee to obtain a work permit. It is issued if the refugee finds a person or company willing to employ him. The prospective employee has to endorse the permit application with a letter to the office of the Commissioner for Refugees in the Ministry of Interior. The Office hands the refugee a form to be completed by the employer specifying the conditions under which he is hiring the refugee, who then takes the form to the Labour Office to be granted the permit.

The problem is that employers generally hesitate to comply with the formalities, for various reasons, including the possibility of employing a refugee at less than the standard wage for the job. 'Since we badly need work, we find ourselves trapped in a vicious circle,' one refugee complained. The Commissioner says, 'We have several times asked prospective employers in general to be more cooperative.' Until they comply, this continues to be a vexed question.

Refugees who want to continue their education, in schools or colleges, also have their problems. Language is the main difficulty. According to the Ethiopian curriculum which was imposed in Eritrea, elementary schools teach in Amharic, and, apart from a few Arabic schools, junior and senior secondary schools teach in English. In Sudan, schools teaching through the medium of English are scarce, and many of them are private. So refugees face the problems both of finding a place and finding finance.

For those who know Arabic, everything is relatively easy. 'What applies to a Sudanese also applies to a refugee,' said a teacher from Piastre Institute where Eritrean refugees, mainly from Gal en Nehal, and Sudanese learn together. Those who do not speak Arabic ask for placement in Comboni schools (in Khartoum, Port Sudan or El Obeid) or Khartoum's Unity High School, where the medium of instruction is English. Obviously, not all of them find vacancies in these schools.

Those who are fortunate enough to do so have the difficulty of obtaining scholarships to support themselves. 'Last year we had to suffer a lot of financial problems because the UNHCR did not help us regularly enough,' said one student.

\*\*\*

## WHO IS PROVIDING HELP?

There are several different refugee organisations. Perhaps the best known is the United Nations High Commission for Refugees (UNHCR) which first came here in 1968 to work with refugees from Ethiopia. In the early 70's, the agency also assisted in the repatriation and rehabilitation of many returning Sudanese.

In Third World countries, the UNHCR provides emergency relief aid when needed, but its main functions are to ensure the safety of refugees and to give them material assistance, either on a temporary basis or, if necessary, to help them attain a position of self-reliance. The goods and funds supplied by the agency are mostly channelled through the Office of the Commissioner for Refugees in the Ministry of the Interior. This office is responsible for transporting and distributing most of the food, tents and other goods supplied by various agencies. Although the UNHCR supplies refugee travel documents to the Government, it is, contrary to widespread belief, the Ministry of the Interior which issues the papers to individual refugees. This was stressed by Mr Anthony Kozlowski, UNHCR Representative in Khartoum. Travelling does not solve the refugee problem,' he said. They are still refugees. He pointed out, however, that many refugees are understandably very keen to go abroad, particularly to the Gulf, where thousands are now working and are thus able to support themselves and their families.

Many of those remaining in the Sudan benefit from the UNHCR programme, directed by Mr Kozlowski and in El Gedaref, by Mr Michel Barton. The programme includes about

965 scholarships and a Local Settlement budget of $2,773.000. The total UNHCR budget for Sudan for next year amounts to $3,591,300.

Also under the auspices of the UN comes the World Food Programme (WFP), which is more commonly thought of as an agency that supplies food linked to local development projects or at times of natural disaster. However the WFP first came to Sudan in connection with the resettlement of 50,000 inhabitants from Wadi Halfa and is therefore familiar with the problems of displaced people. Mr Allam Hassan Allam, who was the Chairman of the Commission responsible for the Halfa settlement, points out that large numbers of Sudanese are therefore experienced in this field. As Director of department of the Ministry of Planning, he is himself now working closely with the WFP and the departments are based in the same building at UNDP head-quarters in Khartoum.

The provision of food to refugees is inevitably a complicated business. One difficulty lies in the fact that the quantity and type of food sent depends on what is available at the Rome head-quarters, according to the UN Adviser to the WFP in Sudan, Mr Noblet. There are also holdups due to transportation difficulties, notably after the foods have arrived in Port Sudan. Where possible, such deficiencies are remedied by consignments supplied directly to the camps by the Sudan Council of Churches.

Necessarily, the basic provisions consist of dry goods, normally wheat, skimmed milk, edible oil, pulses, fish and sugar. In Sudan, the wheat is sold for hard currency and replaced by sorghum, which increases the weight of cereals by 10 to 15 percent. Mr Noblet said this food is supplemented by fresh vegetables and meat given by the UNHCR, although several refugees from Wad el Hillayu claimed that they received no fresh food.

Rumours of refugees starving to death are strongly denied by the authorities on the spot, and in fact, such stories seem to stem solely from dissatisfaction with delayed and inadequate food supplies. For example, 10,000 tonnes of WFP foodstuffs have been standing in Port Sudan since March.

Despite these problems, the WFP remains the major supplier of food to the refugees and since 1967 has given 12,687 tonnes of food, worth $4,235,400, to those from Eritrea and Ethiopia. Food worth a further $1,173,000 has been allocated for settlement programmes.

The UNHCR sends some of its funds to the Refugee Counselling Services (RCS). This is a semi-autonomous organisation formed by the UNHCR, the WFP, the Ministry of the Interior, the Sudan Council of Churches and Sudanaid, and is based in the UNHCR premises in Khartoum. RCS was set up as a joint body in June of last year to avoid duplication of services to refugees living in or passing through the capital.

The staff of four are understandably busy, and work long hours in their efforts to cope with their numerous cases, many of them urgent. They deal with many refugees with specific needs, such as seamen requiring documents to find work at Port Sudan or the mentally and physically handicapped.

RCS also administers a number of scholarships for students in secondary school, university and vocational training, especially in Khartoum and Kassala Province. In cooperation with the Ministry of the Interior and the Labour Office, RCS also helps find food and employment for those who finish their education.

There are also small allocations for refugees who want to return to their countries. RCS has helped several Zairians and Ethiopians to go home, but repatriation is usually the responsibility of the UNHCR. Some South African refugees have been assisted in transit, but at present there are none requiring help in Khartoum.

Apart from its stop-gap food supplies, the Sudan Council of Churches (SCC) also belongs to the RCS, through which it channels financial aid. Its main concern is to provide medical services in Kassala Province, Many of the refugees have been wounded, and Doka and Gedaref hospitals cannot cope with the numbers involved. Between February and April, 14,280 refugees were treated in these two hospitals. Except at times of sudden influx of refugees, those living in Wad el Hillayu seem to be satisfied with the medical services, in fact one resident commented, 'We get more tablets than food.'

The SCC employs two British doctors who work in the camps at Um Gulja, 12 km west of Gedaref and at Um Rakuba. These two camps alone house more than 9,000 people. In addition, these doctors also work at the other four settlements around Showak. There are dressing-stations at Um Gulja, Um Rakuba and Um Gargur. These stations are additional to the normal Government facilities in the Gedaref area: two hospitals, six dressing-stations and six dispensaries. The Commissioner's Office themselves has sent £s6,000 worth of medical supplies over and above those provided by the other agencies.

At the biggest camp, Wad el Hillayu, with its 30,000 refugees, there is a well-equipped pediatric and antenatal clinic which is run and financed by a Swedish church organisation under the auspices of the SCC. Established almost two years ago, the clinic has a doctor, a nurse, a social worker and an engineer. There is a pharmacy, a laboratory and examination rooms, but no facilities for in-patients. Refugees are trained as medical assistants and dressers, as happens elsewhere in the camps.

This clinic is complemented by an out-patients clinic for adults run by the independent West German organisation Asme Humanitas. There is a staff of one Australian nurse, two Eritrean health officers and some dressers. But the problems are not only medical. Morale tends to be low among the refugees, who have lost not only their homes and, perhaps, their friends and families, but also self-respect derived from supporting themselves.

Because the refugees' plight is assumed to be temporary, only short-term projects lasting a year can be set up. These can accomplish a good deal to help the inhabitants, however. Sponsored by the SCC, Dr Katherine Homewood, an anthropologist who is married to one of the British doctors, is organising a weaving scheme based around handlooms which several refugees have brought with them. It is hoped that more looms will be made, as many refugees are skilled in this trade.

Meanwhile in Um Gulya, Dr Jonathan Boyce, in addition to his medical tasks, is directing the construction of latrines. As well as providing work for the residents, this should go a long way towards reducing the risks of epidemics, which are especially great in the rainy season.

The SCC Coordinator for refugees, Mr Damas Deng Ruay, also envisages the provision of some social amenities, including meeting-places for indoor games, eating, watching films and study. Education is, indeed, a major factor in the SCC programme, and 87 students will be sent to various educational institutions here and abroad in the next academic year.

The SCC also suffers from the usual transportation difficulties in supplying goods. 'In terms of food-supply, we are only filling in the gaps,' says Mr Damas. Sorghum, powdered milk, split peas and soya beans have been provided so far, but 272 bales of cloth and 10,000 blankets are held up at Port Sudan.

The same point was made by the Rev. H. Dejemeppe, General Secretary of Sudanaid, which is also a member of RCS. He explained that 100 tents sleeping ten persons each and another ten large tents for stores and administration offices have been waiting at the port for almost two months. These are urgently needed, especially since it has been raining for some time in the area.

Sudanaid has also sponsored some school students in Port Sudan, as well as providing a grinding mill in Kassala Province to save many women the tedious task of crushing sorghum by hand. The association has also contributed $294,650 towards the 1977 budget for refugees in Khartoum.

Founded in Juba in 1972, Sudanaid is part of the Episcopal Commission for Aid and Development, of which the Bishop of Juba, the Rev Vincent Majwock, is president. Its activities are mainly geared to development in the Southern Region, but it carries out emergency programmes when necessary. It has appealed to the Catholic organisation Caritas Internationalis, of which it is a member, for more tents and medical aid.

Medical services are also provided by Eritrean organisations. The ELF and ELF/EPLF each have a clinic at Wad el Hillayu.

The two major liberation fronts each manage humanitarian organisations. The EPLF runs the Eritrean Relief Association (ERA) and the ELF runs the Eritrean Red Crescent and Red Cross Society (ERCCS).

Both Dr Yusuf, ERCCS Chairman and Mr Bitsai Gerense, member of the ERA Executive Board, stressed that they help displaced Eritreans regardless of political affiliation. The two young organisations have won the confidence of international agencies such as the Red Cross and the WCC. The SCC has granted £s3,000 to the ERA and £s250 to the ERCCS.

Most of the work of the Eritrean Relief Agencies takes place within the liberated areas of Eritrea itself, however. It is estimated that there are about 850,000 displaced Eritreans, many of whom are roofless and the victims of hunger and related sicknesses such as anaemia and tuberculosis. In response to this situation, the ERCCS and ERA have built half a dozen hospitals (in caves or excavated under mountains), as well as about 80 clinics distributed more or less evenly around the country.

To meet present needs, as well as those arising from the drought which threatens, both agencies need more funds, which they hope to acquire by appealing to international philanthropic organisations, friendly countries and benevolent individuals. They also hope to enable displaced Eritreans to stay within the liberated areas, where they can retain their sense of identity and play their part in rebuilding the country. However, while the Ethiopian Air Force controls Eritrean air space, many refugees prefer to seek safety in the Sudan.

Those working in the field agree that the Sudan, itself a developing country, has been particularly generous in its treatment of the refugees, both in material terms and in allowing them freedom of movement. It is to be hoped that the hard work of all the agencies involved will only be a temporary measure for, like refugees everywhere, the Eritreans and Ethiopians would certainly rather be able to go home.

\*\*\*

Last year, the UNHCR financed 200 students on one-year courses at vocational schools in Kassala, New Halfa and Gedaref. But the refugees found it hard to adjust to the conditions there, and about 100 of them withdrew one by one. Of those who successfully completed the courses, some are now working in this country, some are still unemployed and others have gone abroad, mostly to Saudi Arabia.

Due to the severe shortage of vacancies in the English schools in Khartoum and elsewhere in the North, a group of about 15 students were sent to continue their studies in the Southern Region, where many higher secondary schools use English as the medium of instruction. Again due to adjustment difficulties, this scheme met a marked look of success. All the students who found schools in the year 1975-76 were financed by the Refugee Counselling Service of the UNHCR. Some who entered the country later found schools, but due to lack of funds were unable to continue their studies. Mr Nasser, head of the Counselling Service, said that there were 21 refugee students in Comboni schools in Port Sudan, El Obeid and Khartoum.

The Commissioner for Refugees recently came up with an idea that could alleviate the problems of those who could not complete their secondary education and are thus unable to go to University. He has proposed the setting up of night schools for 300 students in Khartoum and Kassala.

It is hoped that the UNHCR will be able to finance this scheme, but it is very much a matter for the future. Mr Tony Kozlowski, UNHCR Representative in Khartoum, pointed out 'As a big organisation, we should be approached at least a year ahead. This idea arose only three months ago. But who knows? Somehow we may find the resources to carry it out'.

The Commissioner's Office has already asked the UNHCR for $352,000 to support refugees currently engaged in full-time study. The new night schools would mean an additional $156,000.

Of the 56 Eritrean and Ethiopian students at the University of Khartoum, the IUEF finances 47 and the UNHCR nine. The Sudan Council of Churches was also approached by individual students to finance their education at the University, but as Mr Damas Deng Ruay, Refugee Co-ordinator for the SCC, explained, 'The students applied too late for their applications be duly processed'. However, he added that $20,000 has been earmarked for the next academic year, for students at all levels.

Most of the travel documents issued in Khartoum to Eritrean and Ethiopian refugees have been for onward passage to Jeddah. Refugees can obtain either a passport from the Ethiopian Embassy, or a UN Conventional Travel Document (CTD), or sometimes both. The Ethiopian Embassy gives passports to refugees it recognises as Ethiopian nationals, and has issued about 6,000 over the last two years.

Roughly the same number of CTD's, in fact 5,9000, have been issued over the same period of time by the Refugee Commissioner's Office in the Ministry of Interior.

Mr Kozlowski stressed that, contrary to popular belief among refugees, the UNHCR does not issue CTD's to individual refugees. It is the country granting refugee status that issues them. UNHCR, from its headquarters in Geneva, supplies the countries concerned with the necessary documents on request.

Although in principle every refugee is entitled to a CTD, certain conditions must be fulfilled. The refugee has to have a genuine reason for travel, supported by valid documentary evidence.

Acceptable reasons include scholarships, promise of employment, promise of an accredited entry visa to the country of destination, or an invitation to settle with relatives or friends in the country of destination. It is also important that all refugees have a roundtrip ticket.

In the light of his previous experience in UNHCR offices in West Africa, Mr Kozlowski commented that the Sudan is one of the most liberal countries in the issuing of CTD's.

In spite of, or maybe because of, this policy, the refugees seen lining up in the Ministry of Interior all complain bitterly about the delay in the issue of documents. One said despairingly that he couldn't even get through the gates, let alone present his case to the authorities. Others claim that appointments are not respected, and there are even allegations of corruption that the requisite forms can be obtained speedily if money changes hands.

The Commissioner, however, stresses that his staff are in fact working flat out to cope with the refugees' requirements. Part of the apparent muddle, he says, is due to the tendency of many refugees 'to hang about after they have finished with the formalities, just waiting for their friends, or relatives or to meet new arrivals'.

He said that appointments are kept as promptly as possible, but many refugees come days before the appointment time. In effect the Ministry of Interior is used as a rendezvous, and this interferes with what would otherwise be a smooth process.

Dissensions of this sort are unfortunate, but on the whole relations between refugees, Sudanese people and the Government are very good. Commissioner Omer thinks that in some ways the presence of Eritrean and Ethiopian refugees has had a liberalising influence on some Sudanese attitudes. 'After all,' he said, 'as countries and peoples we already have a lot in common.'

SUDANOW, June 1981

# Easing the burden?

*June 20th is 'African Refugee Day' announced by the Organisation of African Unity and endorsed by the United Nations. Its purpose is to increase public awareness around the world of the continued suffering on this continent of more than five million people, and to motivate yet more fundraising programmes. It comes exactly one year after the International Conference on Refugees in Sudan, and follows in the wake of the International Conference on Assistance to Refugees in Africa, held last April in Geneva. Both conferences were judged to be well-orchestrated and successful, yet little progress has been made towards actually resolving the basic problem. The stream of refugees has in some cases turned into a flood, and the predicament of both refugees and their host countries is becoming ever more complicated. Berhane Woldegabriel looks at the current state of affairs in Sudan, how the aid agencies are operating, and some of the social consequences involved in sheltering refugees.*

OF THE ESTIMATED five million refugees in Africa, 525,000 are being sheltered in Sudan. In Geneva last April, the Sudanese delegation to the International Conference on Assistance to Refugees in Africa (ICARA) reported that Sudan was hosting some 390,000 refugees from Ethiopia and Eritrea, 39,000 from Uganda, 7,000 from Chad and 5,000 from Zaire.

The Geneva conference follows the conference held in Khartoum last June to publicise the refugee situation in Sudan. Perceiving a 'major human crisis, the UN Secretary General -in consultation with the UN High Commission for Refugees (UNHCR) and the Organisation of African Unity (OAU) arranged the ICARA conference to focus public attention on the plight of refugees across the whole of Africa.

ICARA was without doubt a success in that it raised more than the target figure of $500m, in pledged donations. There was a general feeling of sympathy for Sudan, and the delegation's leader – Internal Affairs Minister Ahmed Abdel Rahman Mohamed – expressed the opinion that this sympathy would be manifested in

119

terms of concrete assistance. Of course, a great deal of work has already been undertaken by agencies such as UNHCR, and ICARA will have served mainly to augment the existing programmes of refugee assistance, while alerting worldwide attention to a crisis which compared with the Vietnamese boat people, for example, has so far been under-reported in the international media. Each Asian refugee receives about $50 per year in aid; an African refugee receives $20.

What remains uncertain at present, is the extent of the amount pledged to Sudan. As yet, no one knows how much of the total pledged at the conference will be in cash, and how much will be in relief supplies foodstuffs, medicines, blankets and so on. The donors have not been specific on this matter; moreover, a few donors included aid which they had already provided or announced, when calculating their contributions.

Equally important is the way in which funds are used: it is notoriously easy to spend aid money without achieving effective results. This concern was reflected in the call for aid measures to be coordinated amongst the experienced development agencies.

Last month, as part of its programme to assist the settlement of refugees in Sudan, the World Food Programme (WFP) signed a new agreement with the government to provide food worth $17m. at current prices. The senior advisor to WFP in Sudan, Mr. Gaston Eyben, explained that the aim is to assist the government in its efforts to enable refugees to be self-supporting.

WFP believes that refugees have to participate actively in the economic development of the country of asylum, he stressed, explaining that the idea is to reduce the food aid progressively as the degree of refugee self-sufficiency increases. Exception is made for vulnerable groups those who cannot become self-sufficient through their own efforts, such as the sick, orphaned and the physically handicapped. Under this new programme, 152,000 refugees will move from temporary camps to less temporary settlement areas. The main beneficiaries will be refugees from Uganda, Chad, Ethiopia and Eritrea. There are also some 5,000 Zaireans in the southern Sudan although whether they qualify as refugees is debatable, since they returned to Sudan after having been voluntarily repatriated to Zaire.

'They have been here in Sudan off and on for over fifteen years,' one local official pointed out, 'and they would probably be quite content to stay indefinitely.' Economically speaking, they are better off than the Sudanese in the neighbouring villages. Because of this evident self-sufficiency, it is unlikely that they will be included in the new aid programme.

There has always been migration across the borders: some two million of the present Sudanese population are of Chadian or Nigerian origin, for example. For them, there has been time to integrate. The main difference now is that the rate and volume of influx has increased beyond the normal integrative capacity of the host society.

The World Food Programme's involvement in Sudan is one of its major activities in Africa. Aside from the $17m. resettlement aid, a programme is being conducted with a budget of $75m. covering such diverse elements as youth training, feeding schools, reforestation schemes, rehabilitating railway workshops and a great deal more. In fact, the WFP could be said to have cut its teeth in Sudan: its first ever project was to participate in the transfer of flood victims from Wadi Halfa to New Halfa. Since then, WFP commitment in Sudan has totalled $142m. The $17m. resettlement agreement, although signed last month, was in fact pledged after the June conference on refugees in Sudan held in Khartoum last year: the programme itself is expected to take some three years.

The chief difficulty encountered by the WFP – and other agencies – has always been that of transporting food supplies from Port Sudan to the settlement areas in the hinterland. Although completion of the Port Sudan – Khartoum highway has eased that stage, river transport is still a source of vexation.

'Last February, we arranged a contract with the River Transport Corporation to transport 43,000 bags of dura from Renk to Juba, at the rate of six barges a month, before the start of the rainy season,' explained Mr. Eyben. 'To date, only two barges have made the journey. We have no supplies in Juba for the Ugandan refugees living outside the capital,' he told Sudanow last month.

The inaccessibility of the Chadian refugees also creates difficulties; they are encamped in a region more than two thousand kilometres from Port Sudan, and are dependent on supplies brought by rail via Geneina, or by lorry across extremely rugged terrain. Air freighting has been used, but this, too, has encountered problems (Printout, February, 1980). To help alleviate the situation, an agreement has been reached with Sudan Railways to provide extra wagons for WFP purposes. In the past, there has been a chronic shortage of rolling stock.

Even in the Eastern Region, which has a well-developed infrastructure, refugee camps and settlement areas have run short of WFP staple supplies such as dura, edible oil, beans and milk-powder, while these items turn up in retail shops in the area. In reference to this, Mr. Eyben outlined some of the difficulties inherent in running such a huge operation in a less developed country: 'Once the foodstuff arrives at Port Sudan, it becomes the property of the government. WFP pays half the cost of distribution from Port Sudan to the needy areas, but the periodic food shortages are chiefly due to transport delays. The percentage of WFP goods which find their way into shops is negligible, albeit visible.'

He cited two possible reasons behind this phenomenon. The first is outright misappropriation of supplies – 'Which I don't believe is the case here' – and the second, which he accepts as true, is that 'some beneficiaries prefer cash to one or two of the food items, so after it has been distributed, they sell it to local merchants.'

The WFP imports wheat, but this is usually sold through the Ministry of Commerce and Supply, since the refugees' staple grain is dura. However, according to Mr. Eyben: a ton of wheat cannot buy a ton of dura in exchange. The reason for this is not that the wheat is sold off cheaply, but that the cost of dura is constantly increasing. All WFP consignments are brought in free of duty, except for a provincial tax on the transaction of dura.

The involvement of the United Nations High Commission for Refugees (UNHCR) has increased steadily with the growth of the refugee population in Sudan. Last year it had a budget allocation of $12m. – although actual spending exceeded the amount – and $25m. has been allocated for the current year. 'It seems likely too, that we may end up spending more than that this year,' revealed Ekber Menemencioglu of the UNHCR Information Department.

Unlike previous years, the UNHCR has stopped compiling its own statistics on refugees and their needs, and has accepted the validity of figures issued by the office of Dr. Abdel Rahman Beshir the government's Commissioner for Refugees. The government has more officials at frontier posts and refugee encampments, compared with the number of UNHCR field supervisors, and is responsible for carrying out registration of refugees, distribution of materials and providing security. Asked about the UNHCR's new-found confidence. Dr Beshir replied: 'With more practice, we have naturally improved the efficiency of our own services. Besides, why shouldn't they accept our figures? The other side seems to agree: 'We are here to cooperate with the government in helping refugees, not to contradict it, said the UNHCR's public information officer.

The detailed programme of action for 1982, jointly compiled by the Office of the Commissioner for Refugees and the UNHCR, will be submitted to the UNHCR Executive Committee meeting which will meet next month in Geneva. Mr. Menemencioglu declined to answer questions concerning the content of the programme and the budget estimates for the coming year. We cannot disclose details before the meeting is held, he said.

UNHCR's current projects in the Sudan include the overhauling and improvement of the domestic water supply in Qala en Nahal. Ten years ago, the area had some 20,000 refugees from Eritrea, Now the total population including some 8,000 local inhabitants is 41,000. Financed by the Swedish International Development Agency (SIDA), this renovation work is scheduled to begin in four months time, at the end of the rainy season. The Rural Water Corporation (RWC), whose responsibility it will be, will have until the beginning of the next rainy season to carry out the task. A major pipeline, 36 kilometres long will carry water from two haffirs, or waterholes, beside the seasonal river, Rahad. It will then be pumped through minor pipes up to Salmin, the furthest village. Since the existing two haffirs are exclusively for the human population, the RWC plans to build a third haffir for animals.

A similar water project is being sponsored by the UNHCR in the Gedaref area where there are about 30,000 refugees, mainly from the Ethiopian province of Tigray. Demand for water has increased in recent years as considerable internal migration to the urban area and the continuous influx of refugees has swelled the population. The amount of water obtainable from the pumping station at Showak on the River Atbara has fallen, however, as canals from the dam at Khashm el Girba have silted up and begun to meander. UNHCR proposes to spend $700,000 on repairs and improvements to the present supply system. A water expert contracted by UNHCR from Anglia Consultants told Sudanow that the Showak pumping station itself was a good installation. The generators totalling 920kw and water treatment plant, now ten years old, are still in good working order, according to Mr West. The 72 kilometres of twenty-inch pipeline have been damaged in places by cattle herders seeking to water their animals (and themselves), but elsewhere the pipe is intact.

Similar problems were encountered along the Kassala-Haiya highway when Rashaida herders took matters into their own hands (Development, November 1980). The Italian company Recchi then set an example the water authorities at Gedaref would be well-advised to follow: they installed special haffirs to give the Rashaida proper access to the water. 'Controlling the loss is much better and safer than being stubborn and taking the inevitable risk of having pipes broken which lets a great deal of water just drain away into the swamps,' said Mr. Recchi. It is said that underground water at Abu Nagga, 12km south of Gedaref, could provide a feasible auxiliary to Showak, if necessary. As well as the refugees, the 250,000 local inhabitants of Gedaref will benefit from the UNHCR's project. When the desilting and repairs have been completed, Showak water station will be creating able to pump some 12,500 cubic metres of water in an eighteen hour day equivalent to 50 litres per person.

In addition to assisting the 7,000 Chadian refugees registered in Geneina, the Red Crescent and the UNHCR are taking part in a medical programme aimed at providing the area's 100,000 residents with vaccination against meningitis.

The UNHCR's biggest education programme is to be found in Sudan, claimed their public information officer, explaining that the organisation has been building primary schools, supplying school equipment and supplementing teachers' wages in various parts of the country. In 1980 the UNHCR provided scholarships for 1,250 students in technical and academic secondary education. Two UNHCR schools have also been completed recently: one in Kassala and one in Juba. Each has a capacity of 500 pupils and will be open to both Sudanese and refugee children.

The Sudanese government is uniquely generous in its treatment of refugees, in providing land for settlement,' averred Mr Menemencioglu, going on to say: 'I was in Pakistan with the UNHCR. It is a good country, but the government simply can't help in the same way. It has no extra land to give to the refugees. This is why I object to the use of the word 'camp' here: there are settlement areas in Sudan, but never camps. Refugees can move around the country freely here: in Thailand they are kept in camps surrounded by barbed wire. This is a slight exaggeration: in fact; while land is provided in certain areas, there are still camps without wire at Tawawa and Um Gulja, which differ from Mr Menemencioglu's description.

There are three kinds of settlement: emergency reception areas, agricultural settlements and urban or semi-urban settlements. Emergency reception areas are near the borders, where newly-arrived refugees receive food, medical treatment and protection. Generally, refugees arrive exhausted after long hours or days of walking to cross the border, suffering from both the accumulated stresses of conditions in their home country and the fear of interception in their fight for survival. Agricultural settlements are a more long-term measure, in which a refugee family may receive ten feddans of land to work for themselves, as in Qala en Nahal. Others work as agricultural labourers alongside existing government agricultural schemes such as Es Suki or Khashm el Girba, earning wages by picking cotton or weeding for Sudanese tenant farmers who are sometimes unable to pay them enough to subsist.

Even when refugees have been provided with their own land on which to support themselves, the way the farms operate can present problems. Mahari Solomon and Girmai Ammanuel are refugees from Eritrea, currently in their final year at medical school in the University of Khartoum. As part of their field-work for the university, they spent some time working at Qala en Nahal, which is as established an area for Eritrean refugees as Goz Rejab is for the Zaireans.

The young refugee doctors indicated in their reports that the tractors provided for the settlements by the government are lacking spare parts, even when they manage to obtain fuel. This by itself is characteristic of the country as a whole: less acceptable perhaps is that these tractors are only available to most refugees after the ploughing season has passed. During the season the equipment is often monopolised by non-refugees or those few refugees who have managed to obtain four times the usual allocation of land. This makes it more difficult for the others to be self-supporting.

Refugees of urban origin usually want to settle in the towns, and are thus thrown into competition with Sudanese nationals for limited housing and public utilities. As it is, the rate of internal migration gravitation of people from the rural areas of Sudan towards the towns has accelerated to the point where it is causing problems of security and unemployment. Moreover, their abandonment of the land is leading to the decline of the traditional rural economic sector and reducing the country's Gross Domestic

Product. In times of shortage, it is the refugees who take the blame for overcrowding (Current, October 1979).

'We are used as scapegoats for every failure in the system,' complained Kibrom Taame, a young Eritrean refugee working in town: 'After all, we don't drink petrol. How many refugees have cars? If there is a shortage of bread at the bakery, people complain about us, yet we don't eat bread, we eat home-made injera! If one of us queues for bread, it is most likely a servant, collecting it for his or her Sudanese or European employer. We are thankful that the Sudanese let us live in their country, but for my own part, I don't take a penny from the UNHCR or the government. My brother in Jordan is feeding me, and if the authorities would sell me a travel document, I would immediately leave to join him.'

The Minister of Internal Affairs sees a pattern emerging here: 'It is dangerous to generalise, but on the whole the Eritrean and Ethiopian refugees are mostly young and urban-oriented they prefer to stay in major towns. This adds to unemployment and leads to a rise in house rents. Their lifestyle is also more conspicuous: the attention they attract tends to make them a target for adverse criticism. The Ugandan refugees are less anxious to come to the major towns, and the Chadians are more nostalgic about their homes: they hardly accept the reality of being refugees,' he remarked.

Three days before the arrival in Khartoum of Secretary General Fikresellassie of the Ethiopian Provisional Military Administrative Council (Dergue) for the 12th anniversary celebrations of the May Revolution, several truckloads of Eritrean and Ethiopian refugees from the Three Towns were rounded up without warning and apparently at random. They were detained indefinitely in Omdurman prison. This action emphasises the perceived security risk posed by these refugees, although it is not clear exactly why those who were left at liberty were not also suspect. Nonetheless, with the increasing moves towards rapprochement between Sudan and Ethiopia, the question for many refugees must be: how much longer will they be transported out of the capital or held in

127

detention every time a high-level Ethiopian delegation visits the country?

One attempt to cope with the special needs of urban refugees is the Refugee Counselling Service, which assists with some of their immediate problems and finances scholarships. However, the process is a slow one and only a few refugees could be said to have benefited from the scheme so far.

What does the future hold? Sooner or later it seems, there must be voluntary repatriation or assimilation into the local community. The alternatives of resettlement abroad, or emigrating to work abroad are open to only a privileged few. As far as the rest of the refugees are concerned, it is a question of waiting until suitable conditions prevail in their home country. If their stay is prolonged, however, there is the risk of becoming part of a segregated community without naturalisation: the result is perhaps a ghetto mentality and the social degradation that accompanies it.

Last year, according to government figures, some 4,000 refugees from Ethiopia and Eritrea emigrated; the majority to Saudi Arabia and West Germany. These figures are conservative estimates by some observers, who point out that 3,000 left for West Germany alone.

Refugees who qualify to emigrate are entitled to Conventional Travel Documents (CTD's), which are issued free by UNHCR to government refugee offices and sold to the refugees at a nominal price of seven pounds. If a refugee goes abroad with a CTD and then incurs the displeasure of the country he arrives in, then the original host country, Sudan, is held responsible and must take him back. Consequently references, a sponsor and an entry visa for his destination are necessary before the CTD is issued to a refugee. More than 20,000 CTD's have been issued since 1975. Osman Sabbe, leader of the tiny Popular Liberation Forces of Eritrea, told Sudanow six months ago that there were now about 70,000 Eritrean refugees working in Saudi Arabia, the majority of whom left via Sudan. On the question of voluntary repatriation, Ethiopia claimed at the ICARA conference that 151,000 refugees had returned from various countries: the UNHCR in Khartoum puts the number of returnees from Sudan at around 400.

Following the American Refugees Act of 1980, the US government announced quotas for resettling refugees from various parts of the world in the United States. The quota for Africa for the last fiscal year (October 1980 – September '81) was put at 3,000, one-third of whom are to be chosen from refugees in Sudan. In the previous year about 200 Eritreans and Ethiopians were accepted, and since then a further 350 have been resettled in the United States. The remaining 650 will follow gradually, and the scheme is expected to continue next year, probably at a higher rate. Mrs Jean Kirkpatrick, the United States' UN representative, has said that $11m would be available to help resettle refugees from Africa. This approach to the refugee problem has not pleased the African countries themselves, however, according to West Africa magazine: 'Many African delegates in Geneva... felt uneasy about the US proposal, and the UN High Commissioner, Mr Paul Hartling, said that the UNHCR is not encouraging resettlement for refugees in third countries.'

Although the refugees will have to wait the customary five years to be eligible for American citizenship, they are nonetheless required to sign a document agreeing to register for conscription before they even arrive in the US. This is just a formality really; so far there has not been any conscription as such, according to one rather apologetic American official. The US quota represents one in five hundred (0.2%) of the refugees in Sudan, and strict criteria are applied before selection. Applicants are preferred to have relatives already in the US, and to demonstrate that they risk genuine persecution if obliged to return to their own country.

Applicants are screened initially by the UNHCR branch office. Most sponsored by organisations such as the Lutheran World Service, the U.S. Catholic Federation and the International Rescue conflicts, connected by the American Council of pledging Committee with whom they are Voluntary Agencies. An immigration officer comes to Sudan every two months or so to finalise the arrangements. The refugee is expected to repay only

$250 of the cost of resettlement after he has entered the US and started work.

One official from the Ministry of Internal Affairs said that, in his opinion, the resettlement programme does not help Sudan. First, he reasoned, 'those who leave are the able refugees who could support themselves easily by participating in Sudan's economic development. Those who are left behind tend to be the unskilled, the disabled, the 22,000 sick and the elderly. Secondly, I am afraid that this scheme will attract more refugees to Sudan in the false hope of transit to the American El Dorado. Moreover, this could mean an immense loss of human resources to their country of origin. I am sure that the US government recognises that this is not a permanent solution to the refugee problem in Africa.'

Naturally, the various Eritrean liberation fronts are capitalising on the registration for conscription controversy; and the irony that a refugee who could have fought for his own cause might end up fighting for someone else's. The fronts regard the refugees as potential pools of support, and thus have no wish to see them resettled or assimilated. Of the latter they need not worry: the head of Sudan's Passports and Nationality Office, General Osman Abu Afan, has made it clear that a refugee cannot expect to achieve Sudanese naturalisation.

Africa has half the world's entire refugee population, which must reflect the existence of unpopular governments whose interests do not lie with the interests of their people. Governments which fail to win the support and to the use of sheer force to subdue them and perpetuate their own authority. Too often we are reminded of Lord Acton's pithy remark: 'Power tends to corrupt, and absolute power corrupts absolutely.' When this happens, it is inevitable that those who can, take up arms to fight while those who cannot fight take refuge in neighbouring countries.

It would, however, be unrealistic to lay the blame entirely on tyrannical African leaders.' 'He wouldn't have fallen if he hadn't been pushed,' runs a Tigrinya proverb. Were it not for outside interference, be it the drawing of boundaries for colonial purposes, or the unscrupulous sale of arms to escalate full-scale superpower intervention, there might be no need for conferences, American resettlement programmes and other manifestations of the 'humanitarian's burden'.

As UN Secretary General Kurt Waldheim stressed at the Geneva conference, it is the causes of the problem and not just the effects which need the attention of such conferences.

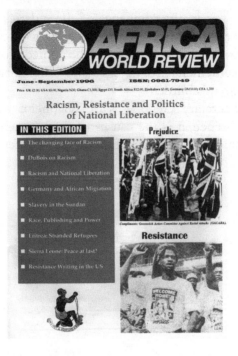

Africa World Review June-September 1996
Eritrean refugees trapped in the same dusty camps in the Sudan

# Refugees who missed the liberation boat still wait

Despite the formal independence of Eritrea in May 1993, the Eritrean refugees in Sudan continue to live as card-carrying second-class citizens in sub-human conditions in camps and settlements, stranded by the political wrangle between Sudan and Eritrea and the perpetual shortage of funds of the ever-stressed United Nations High Commissioner for Refugees, writes Berhane Woldegrabriel.

The situation of ten million African refugees who are currently dispersed round the continent poses a serious challenge to international organisations. In particular, the UNHCR in Geneva and the Organisation of African Unity (OAU) in Addis Ababa need to work out new strategies that could bring about lasting solutions to the apparently insoluble problems that face these refugee communities.

The issue of the half million Eritrean refugees who remain in Sudan more than three years after their country achieved independence illustrates these problems.

The three conventional solutions in the case of long-term refugee settlement have been as follows: The first is to assimilate and naturalise refugees in their host countries. The second, to resettle refugees in 'third countries' (e.g. in the USA and Canada). The third option, which is the most preferred, is voluntary repatriation to countries of origin. The last option presumes that the political or social situation which had threatened their lives and had compelled them into exile no longer exists.

Sudan is the largest country in Africa. In the 1980s, it granted sanctuary to hundreds of Palestinians and to more than 1.2 million refugees from six of its eight neighbouring states. Since then virtually all of the Ugandan, Zairian, Chadian, Libyans and Palestinians have either returned to their respective countries of origin or found themselves other 'third' countries to resettle in. Most of the Eritreans and Ethiopians in Sudan are still there despite the end of the long Ethio-Eritrean war in 1991.

There are around half a million Eritreans in Sudan, most of them in refugee camps.

Clearly the three conventional solutions have failed to put an end to the life of uncertainty and anguish of the 'stateless' Eritreans. Despite the hospitality of the Sudanese people, refugees were used expediently as scapegoats by Sudanese political parties. The 1974 Asylum Act of Sudan prohibits naturalisation of refugees, and prevents them from owning any fixed assets, such as land, houses etc. University education in medicine, pharmacy and engineering was barred to them. Subsequently, refugees remained economically marginalised and political vulnerable.

Formal resettlement of Eritrean refugees from Sudan to the USA, Canada, Australia and Europe, regarded as an option to solve the refugee problem and assist Sudan simultaneously, always fell short of resettling 2,000 people per year. In other words, at that rate, it will take at least 250 years to transport all the estimated half a million Eritreans out of Sudan, assuming that the receiving country continues its willingness to take refugees whose population growth remains constant.

As indicated above, particularly where naturalisation is not permitted and resettlement in 'third' countries is too slow to be viable, voluntary repatriation of the refugees to their home countries becomes the most preferred of the three options. For the Eritreans and many Ethiopians in Sudan and for many others in similar circumstances, such as the Afghans in Pakistan, there must be at least a Fourth Option. The development of this option is primarily the task of the UNHCR, but the refugee units of regional organisations such as the OAU also have an obligation to seek a viable solution to the seemingly intractable refugee problem.

## Sudan, Eritrea & UNHCR

In the political wrangle between Sudan and Eritrea and the perpetual shortage of funds of the ever-pressurised UNHCR, the half of a million or so Eritrean refugees who have been surviving in settlements and camps in distressing circumstances will continue for some more years to come despite the formal independence of their country in May 1993.

Soon after the Eritrean People's Liberation Front (EPLF) set the country and its capital city, Asmara, free from 40 years of Ethiopian occupation in May 1991, the Eritrean refugees in Sudan might have expected that after their long wait they would return home at last. Little did they know that the authorities had agreed that most of the refugees should stay where they were in the hot and dusty semi-deserts of Sudan. After the referendum of 1993, Eritrea became a member of the United Nations and will soon celebrate its third year of formal independence (actually fifth year of liberation), however the refugees are still left to survive in misery, with little hope to look forward to. Three years ago, the UNHCR and the governments of Sudan and Eritrea had signed agreements to systematically and swiftly resettle the exiled Eritreans back in their country. Practically however, the scheme is scarcely in operation, while overtly the three parties are conducting a face saving diplomatic manoeuvre so that the voluntary repatriation programme could appear to be progressing.

## The role of the UNHCR

According to the UNHCR, at the pledging Conference of the Eritrean Programme for the Rehabilitation of Eritrean Returnees (PROFERI), held in Geneva in July 1993, only $32.5 million, nearly half of it in food aid, was pledged by donors out of the requested $111 million for Phase One. The goal of Phase One was to repatriate 'approximately 135,000 returnees to sustainable communities throughout Eritrea. This planning figure includes 100,000 returnees from Sudan who would require repatriation transport as well as integration assistance in Eritrea.'

The start of the Pilot Operation phase which planned to repatriate 25,000 refugees by December 1994 was still more than a few thousands short by May 1995. The delay was 'due to late finalization of the Memoranda of Understanding as well as some logistical problems.' according to the UNHCR 1994-95 report on Eritrea. In March the UNHCR referred to the modification made to the original plan of the Pilot Operation, and stated the reason to be 'unexpected development'.

The UNHCR spent a total of nearly half a billion dollars for refugee programmes in Sudan, which was mainly directed to Eritreans, whose influx into Sudan started as early as 1967. Although it is generally believed that a little over 10% of funds earmarked for refugees actually reach the ordinary refugee in a settlement or a camp, the programmes budget was presumed to have been utilised in building temporary thatched hut accommodation, sinking water wells, erecting primary health centres, elementary schools and grinding mills, and in the construction of a network of summer weather roads in the thirty five refugee settlements in the semi-deserts of Eastern Sudan. About 200,000 Eritreans lived in 30 of those planned settlements either as agricultural wage labourers in the vicinity of large-scale cotton and sugar cane plantations, on plots of land allotted to them by the government of Sudan. Many of them practise pastoralism to supplement their meagre incomes. The remaining 200,000 or so, usually referred to as 'spontaneously settled' live in urban centres, including the capital, Khartoum, without any direct assistance from the Government or UNHCR.

The UNHCR is apparently short of funds, as more and more demands are being put as a consequence of the civil wars in Europe, Africa and the ex-soviet Union. Unless some special funds are allocated by the International Community for Eritrean refugees, the UNHCR as it stands, is unable to earmark the $350 m. which the Eritrean Relief and Rehabilitation Commission (ERRC), calculates is necessary to resettle the refugees back home.

It is more economical for the UNHCR to spend less than $20m annually, to maintain its refugee programme of nearly thirty years in Sudan, than to commit itself to a $350 million operation inside Eritrea. Although it is rightly believed that voluntary repatriation is the most appropriate and durable solution to the refugee problem, such a venture will require of the UNHCR to build some infrastructure for basic health, education and other community services for the returnees. The buildings provided in these circumstances would have to be more durable than those in the refugee settlements.

## The role of Sudan

Across the Eritrean border, Sudan needs the $15.2m. in hard currency that it receives from the UNHCR for the refugee programme. It is already some time since Sudan lost virtually all development (not humanitarian) aid from its traditional donor governments and major international financial institutions, ostensibly for its expansionist Islamist policies.

The impact of the international embargo imposed on Libyan economy following allegations after the Lockerbie bombing has also deprived Sudan of the support of a former ally. Colonel Ghadafi's regime has withdrawn millions of dollars worth of

Libyan money in remittance from Sudan, and has dismissed hundreds of thousands of Sudanese from their jobs and expelled them from Libya during the last quarter of 1995.

However, to the government of Sudan, refugees are not only hostages to be bailed out by the UNHCR, but also a political trump card to manipulate Eritrean policy in favour of Sudan. About 80,000 Eritreans have returned home, most of them from Sudan and without any help from UNHCR. They were supporters of the EPLF which has become the government. Most of those left in Sudan are Moslems and belong to the Tigre, one of the two main ethnic groups in Eritrea. With a resident population of less than three million, Eritrea is a country of nine ethnic groups or nationalities.

According to a UNHCR employee who left Sudan in mid-December 1995, more than 120 Eritrean refugees were arrested by Sudanese security personnel in Kassala town not far from the Eritrean border. The authorities gave no reason to the relatives who dared to ask of the victims for the arrests.

Sudan accuses Eritrea of plotting against it with Uganda and Ethiopia, and with the connivance of Israel and the USA. Eritrea also accuses Sudan of similar conspiracies, alleging that it has used its Islamic fundamentalist influence on the Al Islah party within the Yemeni coalition government, and ignited the Yemen-Eritrean war over Hanish, the Eritrean islands in the Red Sea, in late December 1995.

## The role of Eritrea

The Tigre nationality, generally known as the Beni Amir, has its kin in Eastern Sudan. For most of the war for Eritrean independence from Ethiopia, many of the Eritrean Tigre, who like their Sudanese counterparts are traditionally suspicious of the Abyssinian highlanders, who are Christians (save the Jebertee), were behind the Eritrean Liberation Front (ELF). The ELF predates the EPLF in its struggle for Eritrean independence, but was defeated by a combined force of the EPLF and the Tigray Peoples Liberation Front (TPLF) in 1982. Some of the refugees in

Sudanese settlements were victims of that war and still bear a grudge against the EPLF-controlled government.

In an attempt to accommodate all Eritreans and establish a broader base, the Eritrean government has provided ministerial posts to a couple of ex-ELF leaders and managed to attract some of their followers. Nevertheless, in the advent of Islamic revival, or fundamentalism (depending on how one wishes to view it), some Eritreans have joined the anti-government Eritrean Islamic Jihad (EIJ), an armed organisation. Despite the Sudanese governments emphatic denial, the National Islamic Front (NIF), the party of Dr Hassan El Turabi, which is currently ruling Sudan, is no doubt supporting the EIJ. There are reliable reports that Sudanese security officers have been discouraging Eritrean refugees from returning home, but persuading them to join the Islamist organisation, or any of the relatively secular ELF fronts of Abdella Idris or the ELF-RC, whose leader of 20 years, Mr Ahmed M. Nassir, was replaced democratically in October 1995 by Ibrahim M. Ali.

Eritrea has severed its diplomatic relations with Sudan, and subsequently sued the latter in international forums, such as the Organisation of African Unity (OAU) in Addis Ababa and the European Union – African Caribbean and Pacific countries (EU-ACP) at Brussels. Eritrea has even raised the issue in the United Nations. Since then, Sudanese efforts to strengthen the Eritrean opposition forces from the pool of refugees in Sudan have become overt.

In June 1995 Asmara hosted a conference of all the main Sudanese opposition parties who vowed to oust the NIF government in Khartoum. The Eritrean government is alleged by the Sudanese government of General Omar El Bashir of providing a training camp to the Sudanese Peoples Liberation Army (SPLA) of Colonel John Garang, and radio broadcasting facilities to the National Democratic Alliance, the umbrella organisation for the major Sudanese opposing forces. Eritrea vehemently denies these allegations. President Isaias Afeworki told Richard Dowden, a British journalist, 'We are out to see that this [Sudanese] government is not there anymore... we will give weapons to anyone committed to overthrowing them. Al Mustaqbal, an Arabic paper published in London stated, that President Isaias's statement in the Economist, amounted to 'a declaration of war'.

Another Sudanese allegation which Eritrea dismisses as baseless, is military training provided to members of the Beja Congress Party, yet another opposition to the government in Khartoum. Like the Beni-Amir, the Hadendwa too have their kin (the Hedareb) in Eritrea.

As Eritrea was to Ethiopia an outlet to the Red Sea, the Beja land controls the Sudanese outlet to the Sea. If Khartoum and the rest of the country is cut off from its sea ports of Port Sudan and the ancient Suakin, the government of General El Baashir is liable to crumble, if only through shortage of oil.

If with the participation of the Beja force the Sudanese government fell, the Beja will have accomplished the mission and be redundant in Eritrea. The question is, like the Arab Mujahideen who returned from post-Cold war Afghanistan, the Beja may, like the Afar, (or the pre-1977 Somalia of Siad Barre) entertain the notion of struggling for greater land. But such a Beja land would have to be carved out not only from Sudan, but from Eritrea as well. Their current alliance could become a political time bomb to the power elite in Asmara in a way the Afar on the opposite side of the country are perceived to be.

The Eritrean government, despite its good intentions is not fully prepared to accept the reternees from Sudan for two reasons. First the country has been impoverished by the 30 years war for independence. Four years after independence, it has not yet managed to produce enough food for itself, despite relentless efforts. Thus, a sudden increase in the existing high level of unemployment, by adding a 20% to the current total population may destabilise the government. Secondly, also linked to the destabilisation factor, is the mutual suspicion between the EPLF authorities and the ELF-sympathisers within the returnees. These economic and political risks associated with the return of refugees from Sudan is a liability which Asmara finds it expedient to procrastinate.

## Fourth Option?

It is clear that the UN, the OAU and some international NGOs, are striving to find long term solutions to the root causes of involuntary displacement of peoples through the processes of economic development and conflict resolution. The UNHCR, despite its ever-expanding tasks and limited resources, has shown commendable flexibility when it broadened its mandate to include its active involvement in the rehabilitation process of ex-refugees in the countries of their origin. However, there is still a basic policy problem as illustrated by the situation of the Eritrean refugees in Sudan.

All three authorities to the tripartite agreement in Geneva in 1992 took part in a diplomatic exercise rather than a practical solution. As usual, the loser is the weakest party, the refugees who have hardly any say when their destiny is determined by politicians whose priorities are different from theirs. Do not people in similar predicaments in the world now deserve a stronger UNHCR or perhaps a different institution? The OAU is too poor and the rest of the capable world either is too busy or too indifferent to resolve the problem. The Eritrean official in charge, Dr Nerayo Teclemariam has claimed that his organisation, the ERRC, could transport, resettle and rehabilitate all the half million Eritrean refugees in Sudan within five years, if only he could raise $350m. Is $10m. a year for five years too much to ask from the G7 (world's seven leading industrial countries), especially after their Cold War era involvement in the war in Eritrea left it in economic disaster?

Eritrea is unlikely to speak out for the refugees because, as much as it is aware that it cannot guarantee a decent and sustainable existence for all the returning refugees, and probably thinks that publicising the issue will reflect badly on itself, as there is no legal obligation on Sudan to accommodate refugees who are wishing to return to their country of origin. The USA and particularly the UN, which could have granted Eritrea its independence as early as 1950 and prevented the 30 year war, are responsible for the problem of Eritrean refugee repatriation.

## Islamic fundamentalism

Soon after Sudan declared itself an Islamic State under divine laws (the Sharia), and deliberately undermined democracy and secularism as the bases of 'good governance', development aid was cut, and Sudan was internationally regarded in a negative light. The West views Sudan as a breeding ground and sponsor for strands of Islamic fundamentalism and terrorism. Sudan was thus systematically isolated as a pariah in the society of nations, and was made 'unattractive' to the international media, apart from some favourable representations in the Arabic press. More isolation means less publicity, and subsequently less attention from international organisations. This works against the interests of the refugees who are also suffering from the partial withdrawal of resources by the country.

However, whilst the three conventional solutions for refugee settlement are not working, in an urgent case such as that of the Eritreans in Sudan, it is crucial that the international community renews its humanitarian assistance to Sudan in this respect, whilst still emphasising the need for Sudan to reform its human rights practices. In the meantime, donors of humanitarian aid to Sudan will need to formulate mechanisms that would guarantee the channelling of resources to the refugees more directly as opposed to the mere trickles that currently exist. This strategy would provide a fourth option in the apparent absence of any other workable solution at present.

*This article is dedicated to my friend and colleague Dr. Ahmed A. Karadawi who spent most of his adult life working for and with refugees and died in Sudan in November 1995.*

*Berhane Woldegabriel is a journalist living in London.*

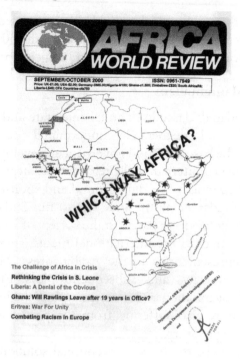

SEPTEMBER/OCTOBER 2000    ISSN: 0961-7949
Price: UK-£1.00; USA-$2.00; Germany-DM5.00;Nigeria-N100; Ghana-¢1.500; Zimbabwe-Z\$20; South Africa/R8;
Liberia-L\$40; CFA Countries-cfa750

The Challenge of Africa in Crisis
**Rethinking the Crisis in S. Leone**
Liberia: A Denial of the Obvious
**Ghana: Will Rawlings Leave after 19 years in Office?**
Eritrea: War For Unity
**Combating Racism in Europe**

Africa World Review September-October 2000

# ERITREA: War for Unity

Like other African states, there is no ethnic group that is unique to Eritrea. The ethnic groups in Eritrea can also be found in the neighbouring states. After independence the Aferwerki government vowed to radically transform the country to the level of Singapore and therefore asked for discipline and loyalty from its citizens. Above all, the government believes that 'national unity is the gateway to self-reliance. It has a mission to achieve this objective but it is Eritrea's neighbours that have had to pay the price of the search for Eritrean national unity. How this objective has been pursued is the focus of this article.

Since the war between Eritrea and Ethiopia began in May 1998, a number of causes have been postulated. The usual ones cited are the boundary issue, the deterioration of economic relations since the launch of the Eritrean currency, the Nacfa, and national pride. While I agree that there is no single cause I also believe that the most important is the issue of national unity because it has two dominant ethnic groups.

The war has emanated from the Eritrean government's desire to fulfill its single most important objective to unify the disparate ethnic groups of Eritrea. The number one and most important of the six goals of the National Programme of the ruling party, the PFDJ (1994) has been National Harmony.

To create a strong Eritrean economy along the lines of Singapore the nine (or ten) ethnic groups must be 'united' and exhibit a level of commitment and dedication similar to the one that enabled them to win their independence.

Before the Italians colonised the area they named Eritrea, at least part of Eritrea was an extension of the Ethiopian empire whilst most of the lowlands looked to Sudan. Throughout thirty trying years, up to independence, the common enemy in the war for survival were the Ethiopian governments of Emperor Haile Selaisse and Colonel Mengistu.

The experience of 60 years of Italian rule, followed by 11 years of British administration engendered the feeling in Eritreans that their exposure to western culture and administrative systems warranted their difference from the rest of that part of Africa. Ironically the colonisers felt (despite the 60 years) that Eritrea was in the same predicament as the surrounding countries. When the future of Eritrea was under debate in the late 40's both the foreign Ministers of Italy and Britain, Sforza and Bevin, proposed the division of Eritrea by uniting the predominantly Moslem lowland area with Sudan and the mainly Christian highland area with Ethiopia. However, this plan was defeated in the United Nations in 1949. After federation, as the Ethiopian grip on Eritrea became increasingly oppressive, the war was in effect a statement that Eritrea was indeed a historical entity rather than a historical accident.

143

The government is well aware of the fragile nature of the unity of the Eritrean State, and quite justifiably the primary aim of the government of President Isiyas, before and after independence, has been national unity.

This objective has been emphasised by the President and members of his cabinet as well as the secretary of Eritrea's only legal party People's Front for Democracy and Justice (PFDJ) at every opportunity at mass rallies and in their statements to local journalists. When the first Eritrean constitution which took years years and $5m to draft was commissioned by the government, Dr Bereket Habtesellassic, the Head of the Constitution Commission, emphasised that the Commission was totally independent and involved more than ½ million people in its deliberations.

'The only advice we received from President Isayas Afewerki,' he admitted, 'was to uphold national unity.'

National unity is also at the top of the PFDJ's programme, implying that the country needs to get united to defeat poverty, disease and illiteracy, which at present is below 20%. Even in peaceful years with good rain, Eritrea has never produced enough food to feed its estimated population of four million (20% of whom are in exile). Contrary to what most Eritreans wish to admit, it is (according to the figures of the World Bank) still one of the 10 poorest countries on earth. The paradox is that Eritreans in refugee camps in Sudan and those on social security in Europe do not like to admit this.

Once, in 1995 I had an opportunity to ask an old school friend, the Eritrean Minister of the Economy (now Foreign Minister) what his main problem was as a minister. Without hesitating, he replied, 'How to convince our people that our economy is starting from zero.' He went on to say, 'I do not know from where we got this idea, maybe we (the EPLF) made them believe it or they formulated it themselves but they seem to believe that our economy will hit the roof in a very short time.' To be fair to the minister, Haile Woldetensae, he was quoted in the local press Hadas Eritrea, as saying that the ousted Ethiopian regime (Dergue) had impoverished Eritrea so much that the Eritrean economy was starting from 'below zero'. What has national unity to do with this? Unconsolidated, Eritrea won the war for independence mainly because of the military competence of the EPLF, and because the fight against the Dergue had 'united' the Eritreans, irrespective of their ethnic, religious and other cultural differences. They resolutely fought together and won. The government of President Isyas Afewerki wants to maintain the same kind of unity and commitment of the people in their fight for economic development. It seems that if the President realised that poverty is not as massive and as real a unifying factor as the ruthless troops of the defunct Dergue. What went wrong?

Eritrea, as mentioned earlier, has been historically divided (like Scotland) by geography into highlands and lowlands, the highlanders in Eritrea, being predominantly Christian (Eastern Orthodox) sedentary farmers, speaking Tigrinya, and looking away from Arabia – some even feel insulted to be referred to as Arabs. Those in the lowlands are predominantly Moslem, Tigré speaking and aspire to be Arabs to the extent that in the drafting of the constitution they fought tooth and nail to make Arabic an official language together with Tigrinya, the de facto official language of United Eritrea.

In order to discourage disparity between ethnic groups, the government proclaimed that there was no such thing as a national language, although during colonial times. Tigrinya and Arabic were both accepted as lingua franca. Instead, under this government, all languages are given equal importance, and elementary education is conducted in the local language, whilst secondary education is in English. Ironically, the effect of this has been to strengthen sub-national cultures on a local and regional basis.

Whilst Tigrinya is the language of elementary education throughout the highlands, the government has refused to include Arabic, which is not the first language of any Eritreans other than the Rashaida and the merchants who have migrated from Yemen, but for centuries has been the medium for Islamic education. It can be argued that one motive for the conflict with Yemen over the Hanish islands was to demonstrate to the people that Eritreans are not Arabs. However, western lowlanders do generally identify themselves as Arabs, and Arabic, which they opted to use during the federation period clearly unifies them as Moslems, and gives a common basis for their relations with their kin in Sudan.

Tigrinya has a common root in the old language of Ge'ez, from which Amharic, a major language of the Ethiopian highlands is also derived, and both are written in the indigenous African script fidel. In the late 1980s, the EPLF made an attempt to replace Arabic script and fidel with a Latin script, in order to create a uniquely Eritrean script (as happened in Somalia). This failed because it was deeply unpopular.

Eritrea is composed of nine or ten ethnic groups, depending on interpretation. All have kin outside the boundaries of the country. They were united in their struggle for independence, but 30 years was not long enough to melt so many ethnic groups into one national identity, particularly as the country is so poor, two of the ethnic groups are equally (50:50) dominant, and the infrastructure is not developed.

Therefore, as soon as independence was achieved and the hitherto common enemy, the Dergue, was removed, these different ethnic communities also started to identify themselves distinctively. Until then, the struggle for independence had overshadowed these distinctions. As a result, the government found it necessary to decide that there would be no political parties based on sub-national identity such as ethnicity or religion. On the other hand, on a local basis, the communities started to contribute on a voluntary basis for local and ethnically based projects. Elementary schooling in local languages bolsters such developments.

The President, who in his guerilla years saw every corner of Eritrea and its people realised that post independence unity is not as cemented as he had wished. So it seems that in order to achieve his dream of a prosperous and developed Eritrea. along the lines of Singapore, an equivalent to the Dergue was necessary as an external threat that would guarantee the unity of the nation, to generate the commitment and stoic perseverance required by the programme for development.

A highly orchestrated and propagated 'Macro economic' policy was laid out in 1996 and expectations were high, as an off-shore oil exploration was also under way on the Red Sea. This may have contributed to the armed conflict against Yemen for what finally became the struggle for the Hanish Islands. This was finally decided by international arbitration, which was settled in favour of Yemen.

Eritrea also engaged in skirmishes on the border of Sudan, in which western lowlanders were mainly deployed against their neighbours, and in a dispute with Djibouti, which involved the Afar people on both sides of the border. Whilst these disputes have been settled, it seems plausible that a strong motivation for engaging in war (at a time when all energies might have been better engaged in development) against its neighbors may have been to carve out an Eritrean identity of those people who have common ethnic and cultural ties in Yemen, Sudan and Djibouti.

Similarly, the border dispute with Ethiopia was intended to enhance the divisions between the highland Eritreans, who are culturally akin to the highlanders of Tigray. Unfortunately, the conflict took a turn that neither side was prepared for, and has been too destructive both in human and financial terms.

After 1991, when the TPLF and OLF in particular stood their grounds to let Eritrea (which was de facto independent) go through an internationally observed referendum, the traditional elite in Ethiopia – predominantly the Amhara – had on the whole, a different opinion. Subsequently, Meles, who is of the same ethnic group as Isyas, was regarded as a puppet of his former guerrilla mentor. Isyas, so much so that he was dubbed the 'Eritrean Ambassador to Ethiopia' by some independent papers in Addis Ababa. So the 1998-2000 war, in effect, brought him to the Ethiopian camp. Not as the Tigrean who was giving unwarranted economic advantage to Eritrea, to the extent that Eritrea once earned more hard currency from the sales of Ethiopian coffee than did its producer, but as the reclaimer of

Ethiopian pride, who had been previously humiliated by plucky little Eritrea. On the other hand. Isyas, who is known for his ability to control circumstances, seem to have miscalculated and, like most miscalculations, it misfired.

The outcome of the war, if at all, is that the Eritrean nation is shaken and traumatised, rather than solidified. According to a friend of mine, Habtegiorgis Abraha an ex-ELF combatant and now a human rights activist, the fact that over 70,000 people crossed to Sudan as refugees instead of going east to the Sahel province, or even to the capital Asmara, clearly illustrates blood and historical ties are stronger than the social machinations of a state. He further noted that despite independence, the EFDJ (the ruling party) has continued to behave as a liberation front rather than a government.

## Eritrea: what happens next?

Presently, Eritrea is inhabited by two types of citizens-former combatants of the EPLF and the rest of the citizens. As the war between Eritrea and Ethiopia involved more than 200,000 troops, the number of first class citizens baptised by war has increased. This new group is now raising questions against the authority.

Once peace is established, a solution could be found to the regional problems in the Horn. Notwithstanding the indispensability of friendly co-operation with Djibouti, Sudan and Yemen, the relations with Ethiopia could be based on mutual exchange of 'idle resources' which they can afford to barter. For example, Eritrea has Red Sea coastline of 1200 kilometres. Therefore, it can afford to allow landlocked Ethiopia access to the coastal area. In return, Ethiopia, which is the aqueduct for the region, could allow Eritrea access to the Tekze river on a reciprocal basis, and systematically irrigate the Ansaba and the Gash Barka regions to ensure food security for the peoples of the two countries.

Any armed organisation worth its salt knows that it can shoot its way to power. As illustrated by State of Chad, today's government could be expelled from political power until it goes to the field as an illegal armed opposition and then shoots its way back to authority. Eritrea has already paid more than enough in blood to entertain this regrettable method. Most of Eritrea's current problems emerged from the government's unwillingness to work with the various opposition groups. It is time for the formation of a national government, consisting of the EPLF/PFDJ and all the opposition organisations. Morcover if armed organisations against neighboring governments (like the National Democratic Alliance of Sudan and the OLF of Ethiopia) continue to operate from Eritrea, and if conflict by proxy replace peaceful dialogue, its meagre resources will be drained and there will be no peace between Eritrea and its neighbours.

**Berhane Woldegabriel**
Freelance Journalist

*To see photocopies of the original magazine articles please visit:*
*https://bit.ly/46rDOEA*

# Appendix 2

## The London Declaration, June 2020

### Joint Declaration of The Eritrean Political Forces

Our country Eritrea achieved its independence and national sovereignty after a long and bitter struggle, during which our people made unparalleled sacrifices. However, their hopes and aspirations were dashed due to the oppressive regime that sat on the reins of power and ruled the country for decades without a constitution and in the complete absence of the rule of law. It is clear to all that the nutritarian regime is leading Eritrea toward disintegration and collapse.

As such, Eritreans have been struggling in various ways manifesting their rejection and resistance to the regime. As part of the long ongoing efforts to unify their efforts in the struggle, the organized political forces were scheduled to meet in London last March 2020 under the sponsorship of the non-profit group 'Eritrean Education and Publication Trust'[35] in UK with the aim of creating a platform for joint action under the theme of 'Salvation of the People and their State'. However, the key agenda items of the conference, that were interrupted due to the Covid-19 pandemic, were successfully discussed and dialogued for over two months via electronic media. The political forces are now pleased to announce to the public their agreement on coordinating their efforts on key common national issues and on the joint work of the opposition forces.

The key driving factors that necessitated reaching this coordination agreement are the following:

---

[35] EEPT

- The urgency of bringing together all Eritrean political forces to respond to the heightened public call for unity to remove the dictatorial regime without delay;

- Betrayals of and threats to Eritrea's sovereignty by the dictatorial regime are glaringly apparent than any time before;

- The worsening of the political and socio-economic crises caused by the failed internal and external policies of the regime are not only increasing the suffering of the nation and the exodus of its youth, but are also endangering the very continuation of the state;

- Equally worrisome and dangerous to Eritrea and its people are the fierce competitions of the regional and international powers that is prevailing in the region.

This agreement, which has been reached with earnest determination and sense of responsibility of the signatory organizations, is highly expected to be an important chapter in the struggle of the Eritrean opposition forces.

## 1. Objective of Coordination Process

To remove the autocratic regime and replace it with a constitutional and democratic system of governance, it is imperative that the Eritrean political forces identify key areas for joint serious actions. It has been learned from the past years' experiences that the protection and promotion of our people's unity, national sovereignty and guaranteeing human rights primarily requires common action in a unified manner. With this understanding, we are resolved to work to develop a joint strategic plan for our struggle to achieve the aspirations of our people, and to accelerate the pace towards the overthrow of the dictatorial regime.

Taking into consideration the above stated facts, the signatories of this document agree as follows:

a) Engage in continuous dialogues, work diligently and conduct necessary studies related to the establishment of a broad political coalition of all opposition forces;

b) At the same time, carry out joint and coordinated action plan in the various fields of struggle by forming the task forces listed below;

c) Contribute the human and material capabilities to set up the task forces entrusted with the implementation of the agreed joint action plan;

d) To enable the joint task forces to be effective in their areas of action, a coordinating committee shall prepare a detailed directive for implementing the joint action plan without hindrance, and the task forces are accountable to the coordinating committee.

## 2. Establishing the Coordination Committee and Task Forces

To face the ongoing danger to our national existence, there is a need for establishing a coordination committee to guide and administer joint operations through task forces created to act on the various fields of joint actions. To make it more effective, the Coordinating Committee will primarily consist of persons selected based on their competencies and capabilities, but also shall reflect the diversity and capacity of the constituent parties. Within this process of joint work, it is important to encourage our political forces to consider unification with organizations of similar political programs when possible.

### a) Coordination Committee

The Coordination Committee shall be formed by the parties signing this agreement. Committee members shall perform their duties diligently and reach decisions through consensus. This committee is responsible to guide the actions of the task forces and shall be coordinated by its chairperson selected from among its members.

## b) Task Forces

Task forces shall be formed and deployed for action immediately after this agreement is put into effect. Competence and capability are the key factors for assignment of persons to the various task forces. Their work shall be limited to their area of assignment.

## c) The selected fields of action for Task Forces

1. Diplomacy
2. Media
3. Mass Mobilization
4. Intelligence and Information
5. Other areas of joint action as deemed necessary in the future.

## d) Time Frame

The Coordination Committee shall be established within 30 days, and the Task Forces within 60 days as of the date of adoption of this agreement,

## Names of the political coalition/front/organization

Eritrean National Council for Democratic Change (ENCDC)
Eritrean National Front (ENF)
Eritrean People's Democratic Party (EPDP)
Unity for Democratic Change (UDC)
United Eritreans for Justice (UEJ)

**Long live to the Eritrean People with their rights and liberties preserved!**
**Death to the Dictatorial regime in Eritrea!**

**June 2020**

See the original document with signatories at:
https://encdcnet.files.wordpress.com/2020/06/eng.-joint-declaration-of-eritrean-political-forces-june-272020-final-final.pdf

# Essay by Tekeste Negash

*Dedicated to Berhane*

## A biography of Eritrea through six generations from 1890 to 2020

### The synopsis

A generation is usually considered to be about 30 years (in Europe), a period that it takes for children to grow up and become adults and have children of their own. The term generation also refers to all people born and living at about the same time. From its creation and up to the present Eritrea has produced five generations, each of which produced legacies, some positive and some negative.

The project that I wish to undertake would follow the methodological parameters of a biography (for instance a biography of Ibrahim Sultan or Bahta Hagos), but the biography of a society would put more emphasis on the actions and intentions of the section of the population which, owing to its generational position, exercises power over the society at large.

The overarching question that permeates the study is the following: What has a generation (let us say the second generation) inherited from the earlier generation and what values has it (let us say to the second generation) transmitted to the succeeding generation? There is always something useful transmitted from one generation to the next. While the intensity of what is transmitted varies from society to society as well as from generation to generation, the chain of transmission is not always smooth. Calamities (such as civil wars, severe climatic changes, etc.) new technologies and innovations may affect the quality and quantity of what is transmitted from one generation to the next.

This study of the biography of Eritrean society shares many similarities with other modern history books in so far as it bounded by time and space; yet it is different because it pays more attention to the institutions (governance, education, culture, and religion) that display aspects of being inherited (from earlier generation) and would be passed (what and how much are the interesting questions) to the succeeding generation.

Six generations have gone from the time of Italian colonisation of Eritrea in 1890 to the publication of the most insightful book of Bereket Habte Selassie (*While waiting or working for change: things to do and pitfalls to avoid in Eritrea,* Red Sea Press, 2015) where he discusses the deplorable conditions of the fifth and sixth generation.

Here below I shall outline the major features of each generation, but I shall put major emphasis on the sixth (last) generation.

In January 1890, Italy consolidated its disparate possessions (the Afar in the South and the Beni Amer/Hadendowa in the north and the highlands in the south and southeast) into a single colony and named it Eritrea. So for the sake of convenience we can take the generation that was put together and given a new name – that of Eritreans – as the first generation. Indeed, it has to be noted that at the initial period of Italian colonialism, the Eritrean society like any other society in the world, was multi-generational; there were grandmothers, fathers and their children, most of them sharing the same compound. Yet one can state that the generation that confronted the brunt of Italian colonialism at first encounter (1890-1900) were those who were between 18 and 40 years old.

Characteristic of the first-generation Eritreans was the severe experience of the Great Famine that first struck Eritrea, then Ethiopia and then the entire Rift valley reaching Mozambique. The Great Famine started in 1888 and lasted until 1892. Ironically enough, the great Famine was caused by Italian imports of horses from India to Eritrea soon after the Italian occupation of Massawa in 1885. The infected horses from India in turn infected the livestock of the entire Eastern Africa and thus deprived the people of their plough oxen. It is estimated that the pest (known as the rinderpest) killed up to 90% of the livestock in Eritrea and Ethiopia. Unable to farm their lands, people became very hungry and hundreds of thousands of them fled to wherever they can procure something to eat.

Italian occupation of Eritrea, and especially of the Eritrean highlands took place with virtually no resistance from the Eritrean people. Eritrean society was much weaker in 1890 compared to what it was in 1885-87. We need to recall the resounding victory that Ras Alula, heavily relying on Eritrean and Tigrean forces, scored against Italy where; he ambushed and killed 500 Italian soldiers at Dogoali – few kilometres from Massawa on January 26, 1887.

The great famine sapped the energy of many Eritreans to fight against the encroaching Italian colonialism. The Italians brought food with them and hence could easily persuade people to collaborate with them. The newly established Ethiopian government further supported and encouraged Italian occupation of Asmara and the surrounding districts thus further legitimating Italian presence in Eritrea. Ethiopia of the period (that is under Emperor Menelik) knew very little and cared less of what happened in the rest of the so-called Eritrean region outside of the highland districts. This was in sharp contrast to the geographical and political awareness of Emperor Yohannes, 1872-1889.

The second-generation Eritreans were those that we can describe as the Tripoli generation – a generation which came to age around 1915. Italian colonialism was deeply rooted, and the Eritrean generation of the period had by and large accepted its fate as subjects of Italy. From 1912 until 1932, successive cohorts of Eritreans served as *askaris* (or colonial soldiers) in Italy´s wars of conquest of Cyrenaica and Tripoli (which eventually became

157

Libya). The colonial economy was good; famine was avoided and askaris (Eritrean soldiers under Italian colonial rule) emerged as urban pioneers. Farm plots of Askaris were worked by labourers who migrated from Tigray and northern Ethiopia.

The Libya/Tripoli generation took a great deal of pride; they were aware that they were the backbone of Italian army overseas. There were few dissenting voices but were buried under the military fanfare of the combined Eritrean and Italian forces.

The second generation handed a value to the succeeding generation, namely that of being a solider and that a military career led and financed by Italy paid quite well.

The third-generation matured during the Italian Invasion of Ethiopia in 1935. Indeed, up to 60,000 Eritreans (probably as many as 35% were from western and eastern parts of Eritrea whereas the great majority were from the highlands) were conscripted to fight beside Italy and against Ethiopia.

The third-generation produced more dissidents (who opposed Italian colonisation of Ethiopia) than the earlier generations of Eritreans. The third-generation was the one that, on the aftermath of the defeat of Italian colonialism, campaigned for the immediate union of Eritrea with Ethiopia. This generation was in power throughout the 1940´s and 1950's. It was most probable that the racist ideology (put into practice in Asmara and other urban areas), the impressive/charismatic personality of Emperor Haile Selassie, and the pledges that the British Military administration had made to the Eritrean people had created a most favourable climate for a new politics of Ethiopian nationalism. It is therefore plausible to argue that the external factors were of decisive importance rather than what was inherited from the second-generation.

The most outstanding accomplishment of the third generation was the union of Eritrea with Ethiopia, de-facto in 1952 and de jure ten years later.

The fourth-generation, unlike earlier generations, was split in half – the parents who fought for union with Ethiopia remained fast to their beliefs while their daughters and sons begun the process of selective memory of the past where the transitional decades of the late 1940's and up the end of the 1950s were captured as fine moments. The fourth-generation was the greatest beneficiaries of both Italian/British colonialisms and Ethiopian policies of integration. The fourth-generation made its debut in early 1960's and played a major part in the formation and evolution of Eritrean liberation movements (in Eritrea) and that of the Ethiopian student movement in the capital of the Ethiopian Empire.

The fourth-generation, like its Ethiopian counterpart was caught up in the cold war that started in the 1960's and ended in just 1990. Marxist and/or Maoist ideologies had the upper hand in the political formation of the fourth-generation.

The fourth generation carried within its womb, so to say, two groupings; those who supported the old regime (the Imperial system) and those who were effectively indoctrinated in ideologies developed for other societies elsewhere. The political expression of the fourth-generation was the capture of the Ethiopian state by the military junta in Addis Ababa and on the opposite pole the emergence of the Eritrean People's Liberation Front as the only dominant organization in 1981.

The fourth-generation succeeded to break Eritrea away from Ethiopia. The fourth generation implemented the wish of those Eritreans (heavily supported by Italy and Italian interests) who fought for the independence of Eritrea. The fourth generation rejected the dominant views of those (in the third generation) who fought for the immediate and unconditional union of Eritrea with Ethiopia.

The fifth generation made its entry in 1991 with the independence of Eritrea and the regime of EPLF/PFDJ. It took a decade and a meaningless war for the fifth generation to realise that Eritrea and

159

its past are a burden rather than a resource. Ruled by a party that has neither trust nor faith on its people, this generation has chosen to abandon Eritrea. What is happening in Eritrea (mass outmigration that started in 2003) has few parallels in the world; Venezuela might be comparable.

Eritrean society has never been as weak as during this fifth generation. Perhaps, one can draw some parallels with the first generation and its encounter with Italian colonialism. The fifth generation is under the hard clutches of the fourth generation. Eritrea is still ruled by the people who were politically and ideologically socialised during the Imperial period, 1962-74.

As the decade of 2020 unfolds, the sixth generation is coming of age. What has the sixth generation inherited from the earlier generation and what new inputs would this generation make as it marches from the present into the future? That is the question that is legitimate to raise but not easy to answer as both the future and human action are highly unpredictable.

So far and to my knowledge the only person who has devoted some thought to the close links between the course of history and the generation that bears it, is Bereket Habte Selassie, *While waiting or working for change: things to do and pitfalls to avoid in Eritrea,* New Jersey: Red Sea Press, 2015. A conference held in Pretoria, May 9-11, 2014. Allow me to use an extensive quote from Bereket as a background for detailed discussion on the makeup of the sixth generation. I quote:

> The vast majority of the members of the diaspora are the escapees of the last ten years. Their epic story is testimonial to the human spirit – to courage, determination, persistence and ingenuity – a characteristic that defines Eritreans. A few of these heroic escapees have joined one more of the political parties, some have joined civic organizations. The vast majority remain outside of the groups, tending to go with the flow and concerned with daily problems of survival, and wishing to

forget the harsh life that they left behind. Many indeed express extreme sentiments about their experience and do not want to be reminded of it or even of Eritrea. They boldly assert that they have amply paid their dues and tell recruiters of political parties or civic organizations to spare them preaching about nation and people, which to them sounds utterly sanctimonious. They are bitter and it is anybody's guess as to whether they can be eventually induced to recover their faith in the nation they left behind. Many seem to see their future in their adopted country of refuge, not in the nation they left behind. This is indeed one of the saddest aspects of the current Eritrean reality. It raises some serious questions with deeper implications for Eritrea's future (2014:33-34).

To what extent and how much is the mental/cultural makeup of the majority of Eritrean diaspora that Bereket Habte Selassie explained reflection of the mental/cultural makeup of the youth still languishing under the national/military service inside Eritrea? Good evidence is hard to come by but there are sufficient indicators that there is a very strong desire among the youth in Eritrea to leave the country and join the growing population of Eritrean escapees in the Diaspora. One of the main reasons for the closure of the Eritrean/Ethiopian border (only six months after the agreement of September 2018) was the real fear of Eritrean outmigration to Ethiopia.

Bereket Habte Selassie puts heavy burden on the shoulders of what he called 'the millennial generation and those immediately above them in age that were in their teens when the nation was born out of the heat of armed struggle' (2014:33). Bereket Habte Selassie is referring to the fifth and sixth-generations (those who matured in early 1990s and those who matured in the new millennium, that is after 2000). Bereket is convinced that Eritreans are facing an 'impending danger – the possibility of losing forever a once promising nation' (2014:34).

161

Bereket Habte Selassie (a 90 years' old robust gentleman) embodies several generations. He was a major player in the late 1950s and early 1960s as an ardent Ethiopian. He caught up with the fourth generation of Eritrean soon after the downfall of the Imperial system (from mid-1970s) and strode the streets of Asmara together with President Isaias Afwerki in the early 1990s. After serving President Isaias and his system for over a decade, he managed to keep himself abreast of the new times and joined (autumn 2000) Eritrean opposition in the diaspora. He retired from active politics when he was in his eighties. His concluding remarks are indeed insightful into the workings of generations:

> I address this urgent call especially to the members of the millennial generation and those immediately above them in age that were in their teens when the nation was born out of the white heat of armed struggle. Will you, and we your elders, remain as mere observers while our nation gradually disintegrates or will you become its saviours.

An aspect that Bereket Habte Selassie did not raise is the legacy of what we can call the governance system of President Isaias and his party on the sixth generation. According to Bereket Habte Selassie (2014:5), 'the militarization of society has resulted in a brutalized captive population, as a result of these conditions, there has been social and economic dislocation, including the disruption of educational and career opportunities of an entire generation of Eritreans'.

A radical overhaul of the governance system put in place by Isaias Afwerki and his political party is indeed a precondition for the painstaking work of rebuilding the confidence of the sixth generation and their successors. However, as governance systems tend to outlive the people or organizations that create them, the passing away of President Isaias Afwerki (ruled since 1971) or the change of his political system would not necessarily usher new political culture.

What can civic organizations such as the EEPT (Eritrean Education and Publication Trust) do in terms of reaching out to the sixth-generation Eritreans and engage them in the complex process of remembering useful values, forgetting and or rejecting repressive traditions and imagining different futures?

\*\*\*

In the autumn of 1963, I joined Prince Mekonnen Secondary School in Asmara. Berhane Woldegabriel was, also in the same school but he was two grades up. I left Asmara for Jimma in 1964. I met Berhane for the second time in Amsterdam in 2000. He had no problem in recognising me because, as a chairman of a small gardening club I had the privilege of putting to labour (for one full hour) all those who came late to school. Those who were in grade 10 and 11 had very hard time being bossed by a bunch of ninth graders who, out of boredom built a club and were rewarded by Mr Paul, the director, to have free labour.

I knew that Berhane was connected to SOAS (University of London) and was involved in the Eritrean Education and Publication Trust. I did not get in touch with him simply because I was very busy managing work and family. In the early spring of 2019, I met Berhane Woldegabriel by accident on the streets of London (in front of Brixton tube station). He informed me about the EEPT and asked me to give a lecture the next time I came back to London. By then, as a retired academician I had plenty of time in my hands and I was extremely happy of our encounter.

On August 24, 2019, I gave a talk on the prospects for good relations between Eritrea and Ethiopia. On October 14, 2019, I applied formally to join the Eritrean Education and Publication Trust. In a letter dated October 18, 2019, Berhane informed me that the members of the Board accepted me as a member of the EEPT. I met Berhane for the last time on early February 2020. He invited me to deliver a lecture on a book project on a biography of Eritrea through six generations. I had conceived it as a collaborative project between me and the EEPT but then came first the Covid pandemonium and the premature death of Berhane in November 2020. I dedicate this paper to the memory of Berhane – a very generous friend with an equally generous heart.

*Tekeste Negash is Professor of History, Uppsala University, Sweden.*

# Index

BV - #0003 - 121023 - C26 - 210/148/10 - PB - 9781914151927 - Gloss Lamination